The Last Week of Jesus

Keith A. Butler Sr.

Unless otherwise indicated, all Scripture quotations in this volume are from the *King James Version* of the Bible.

Scripture taken from *The Amplified Bible*, Old Testament copyright © 1965, 1987 by the Zondervan Corporation. The Amplified New Testament copyright © 1958, 1987 by The Lockman Foundation. Used by permission.

First Printing 2000

ISBN 1-893575-17-9

Word of Faith Publishing
20000 W. Nine Mile Road
Southfield, MI 48075-5597

Contents

Chapter 1
The Beginning of the End

The Lord Jesus Christ came to the earth as a babe born of the virgin Mary (Matt. 1:23). The Word of God says that as He grew, He *"...increased in wisdom and stature, and in favour with God and man"* (Luke 2:52). Then Jesus had a ministry on earth that lasted approximately three years before He was crucified.

Today Jesus, the Risen Lord who's seated at the right hand of the Father, still has a ministry on earth. But His ministry as He walked the earth in the flesh is what is commonly referred to as His *earthly* ministry. That ministry had a definite beginning and a definite ending.

In this book, we want to take a close look at the last week of Jesus on earth. For example, have you ever wondered what happened during the last seven days of Jesus' earthly ministry — what He taught?

Throughout Jesus' three-year ministry on the earth, everything He taught was important. But, usually, a teacher brings out his most important points at the end. As a teacher of the Word of God myself, I always bring out my most important

1

points at the end of my teaching. I understand that what I say at the end is probably what the people will remember most.

So let's take a look at Jesus' last week and see what it was that He ministered during His last few days on the earth.

Jesus Enters Jerusalem Triumphantly

Palm Sunday is the recognition of the day one week before what we call Easter Sunday — the day we celebrate the resurrection of the Lord Jesus Christ. Palm Sunday commemorates when Jesus entered Jerusalem triumphantly. Let's read about His entry into Jerusalem.

MATTHEW 21:1-3,6-9
1 And when they drew nigh unto Jerusalem, and were come to Bethphage, unto the mount of Olives, then sent Jesus two disciples,
2 Saying unto them, Go into the village over against you, and straightway ye shall find an ass tied, and a colt with her: loose them, and bring them unto me.
3 And if any man say ought unto you, ye shall say, The Lord hath need of them; and straightway he will send them. . . .
6 And the disciples went, and did as Jesus commanded them,
7 And brought the ass, and the colt, and put on them their clothes, and they set him thereon.

8 And a very great multitude spread their garments in the way; others cut down branches from the trees, and strawed them in the way.
9 And the multitudes that went before, and that followed, cried, saying, Hosanna to the Son of David: Blessed is he that cometh in the name of the Lord; Hosanna in the highest.

This passage is referring to Palm Sunday, which marked the beginning of Jesus' last week. For the most part, Matthew, Mark, Luke, and John all recorded the same events. But it is a fact that every person sees different sides and, therefore, emphasizes different aspects of what he sees. For example, if a certain incident occurred in front of a large church, all the thousands of people of that church might witness the incident. Yet if the police took statements from each person, they would find some variations in the statements. All of the statements might be true and right; they would consist of what each person saw. But each person would see the incident from his own vantage point.

The same thing is true with the Gospels of Matthew, Mark, Luke, and John. Each writer recorded what he saw from his vantage point.

Let's read Mark's account of Jesus' entry into Jerusalem.

MARK 11:1-3,6-9

1 And when they came nigh to Jerusalem, unto Bethphage and Bethany, at the mount of Olives, he sendeth forth two of his disciples,

2 And saith unto them, Go your way into the village over against you: and as soon as ye be entered into it, ye shall find a colt tied, whereon never man sat; loose him, and bring him.

3 And if any man say unto you, Why do ye this? say ye that the Lord hath need of him; and straightway he will send him hither. . . .

6 And they said unto them even as Jesus had commanded: and they let them go.

7 And they brought the colt to Jesus, and cast their garments on him; and he sat upon him.

8 And many spread their garments in the way: and others cut down branches off the trees, and strawed them in the way.

9 And they that went before, and they that followed, cried, saying, HOSANNA; BLESSED IS HE THAT COMETH IN THE NAME OF THE LORD.

In verses 1 through 3, we find that Jesus was about to make His entrance into Jerusalem. He knew He was going to ride into Jerusalem in triumph. He also knew what was going to happen a few days from then. Those very same people who would shout, "Hosanna" and lay their palm branches and garments on the ground as He came in would stand before Pilot and say, "We don't know the Man. Crucify Him!" (Mark 15:13,14).

Jesus knew He would be stretched on that Cross between Heaven and earth. He knew He was about to be crucified. But before that would happen, He would make a triumphant entry into Jerusalem.

Jesus' VIP Transportation

Jesus told the disciples that there was a colt which no man had ever sat upon. He told them to go get that colt. Why did He do that? Why did He tell them to get this colt that had never been used?

Today, of course, we wouldn't use a colt to enter a city; we wouldn't use that mode of transportation. We would say, "Go get me a brand-new car, not a used one."

You see, God always has the best, and He doesn't settle for anything less! That was His will for Jesus, and that's what God wants for His people today. God's perfect will for His people is that they come to the place where they have everything new. God wants you to have new clothes, a new house, and a new car that nobody else has had before!

When Jesus gave the disciples their instructions, they said to Him, "Well, when we get this colt and untie it to bring it to You, they are going to stop us. What are we to say?" Jesus answered, "Tell them that the Lord has need of it" (Mark 11:3).

The Lord doesn't want your leftovers. No, He wants your best. He wants your best years. He doesn't want you to wait until you get old before you decide to serve Him. Serve Him while you are the age you are now. God wants your best in everything you have. He has need of what you have to finish His work.

The disciples of Jesus put their own clothes on that new colt for Jesus to ride on (Mark 11:7). They took off what they had on and prepared the colt for Jesus to ride into Jerusalem triumphantly. The disciples understood that they should take what they had and give it to the Lord for His final service.

Let's continue reading what happened in the final moments of Palm Sunday.

> **MARK 11:8-11**
> **8 And many spread their garments in the way: and others cut down branches off the trees, and strawed them in the way.**
> **9 And they that went before, and they that followed, cried, saying, Hosanna; Blessed is he that cometh in the name of the Lord:**
> **10 Blessed be the kingdom of our father David, that cometh in the name of the Lord: Hosanna in the highest.**
> **11 And Jesus entered into Jerusalem, and into the temple: and when he had looked round about upon all things, and now the eventide was come, he went out unto Bethany with the twelve.**

Remember, this was Jesus' last week. Some could sense that this thing was coming to a head. There was an air of expectancy and excitement. The anointing was building as the consummation of God's plan drew nigh. It was the beginning of the end of Jesus' last days on the earth.

Chapter 2

The Law of Faith:
One of Jesus' Last Teachings

We just read that Jesus made His entry into Jerusalem on what we call Palm Sunday. It says, *"And Jesus entered into Jerusalem, and into the temple: and when he had looked round about upon all things, and now the eventide was come, he went out unto Bethany with the twelve"* (Mark 11:11).

Let's pick up from there by continuing in Mark chapter 11.

> **MARK 11:12-14**
> 12 And on the morrow, when they were come from Bethany, he was hungry:
> 13 And seeing a fig tree afar off having leaves, he came, if haply he might find anything thereon: and when he came to it, he found nothing but leaves; for the time of figs was not yet.
> 14 And Jesus answered and said unto it, No man eat fruit of thee hereafter for ever. And his disciples heard it.

For the sake of discussion, Jesus made His triumphant entry into Jerusalem on Sunday. Verse 12 says, *"And on the morrow...."* That means that on Monday, Jesus was on His way to the temple from Bethany when He walked by the fig tree (v. 13). He saw no figs on the tree and did something strange: He talked to the tree. He said, *"…No man eat fruit of thee hereafter for ever…"* (v. 14). Then He went into the temple in Jerusalem (v. 15).

Let's read Matthew's account of what happened at the temple.

> **MATTHEW 21:12-14**
> **12 And Jesus went into the temple of God, and cast out all them that sold and bought in the temple, and overthrew the tables of the moneychangers, and the seats of them that sold doves,**
> **13 And said unto them, It is written, My house shall be called the house of prayer; but ye have made it a den of thieves.**
> **14 And the blind and the lame came to him in the temple; and he healed them.**

When Jesus went into the temple and threw over the tables of the money-changers, He threw out all the animals that were sold for making sacrifices. He threw out all the merchandising that was going on. Then He called in all those who were sick, blind, and withered, and He healed them all. What was Jesus doing? He was cleaning out the temple from all the things man was doing and began using the temple for its proper purpose, which was to minister to the people of God.

Clean Up Your Temple!

You need to understand that today your body is the temple of the Holy Ghost. First Corinthians 6:20 says, "*. . . glorify God in your body. . . .*" It also says that your body is now the "church building" of the Holy Ghost (1 Cor. 6:19), and God wants you to clean that place up! He doesn't want you stuffing it with things that can kill it or prostitute it. That is why God is against smoking, drinking, illicit drugs, and everything else that would defile your body.

Your body is a holy temple. It should be ready so that the anointing of God can come on you, and your body can be used to minister to people. God wants to use your house to minister to the sick. Mark 16:18 says, "*. . . they shall lay hands on the sick, and they shall recover.*" Your body is to be used to preach the Gospel of the Lord Jesus Christ.

So Jesus went into that temple in Jerusalem and cast out everything that didn't belong there. Matthew's account says that He ministered to those people, and then He left the temple and went back to Bethany.

Let's pick up the story, reading from Mark's account.

MARK 11:20-22
20 And in the morning, as they passed by, they saw the fig tree dried up from the roots.

21 And Peter calling to remembrance saith unto him, Master, behold, the fig tree which thou cursedst is withered away.
22 And Jesus answering saith unto them, Have faith in God.

Notice what teaching Jesus reserved for the last. He knew that fig tree was there. He passed by it on purpose. Jesus knew exactly what He was doing. He was coming right down the stretch, toward the end of all things. And what lesson did He want us to learn during that last week — between Palm Sunday and the day of Easter when He would rise from the dead? *He wanted us to learn the lesson of faith.*

You Can Trust God

Peter noticed the fig tree withered. He remembered that Jesus had cursed it on His way into the city. Jesus said to Peter, "Have faith in God."

You need to understand that you can trust God. Whatever your problems, whatever your situations, whatever your circumstances — you can trust God to see you through them. He will! That is, if you put your confidence in Him.

What do you have to do to receive from God? You have to curse what is not producing. The fig tree wasn't producing and Jesus cursed it. If your body, for example, isn't producing, speak the Word of God to it. If your money isn't producing, tell it, "You are dead, and now something alive is going to come from you" (John 12:24). Jesus spoke to that fig tree, and it dried up from the roots. In other words, the problem dried up and withered.

Isaiah 54:17 says, *"No weapon that is formed against thee shall prosper; and every tongue that shall rise against thee in judgment thou shalt condemn. . . ."* This verse didn't say that God would condemn it for you. *You* are to stand up and condemn it. In other words, you tell the problem or circumstance that it's not going to have its way — that it can't win against you — because anything that comes against you will not prosper. Why? The rest of Isaiah 54:17 says, *". . . This is the heritage of the servants of the Lord, and their righteousness is of me, saith the Lord."* Your righteousness is of the Lord!

The Law of Faith

Let's continue reading in Mark chapter 11.

MARK 11:23
23 For verily I [Jesus] say unto you, That whosoever shall say unto this mountain, Be thou

removed, and be thou cast into the sea; and shall not doubt in his heart, but shall believe that those things which he saith shall come to pass; he shall have whatsoever he saith.

Notice that one of the last teachings of the Lord Jesus Christ was about the power of words. *Faith-filled words dominate.* Jesus said that if you believe in your heart and you speak to your mountain, telling it to move, it will move! So tell the mountain of poverty to move if that is your mountain. Tell the mountain coming against you — whatever it is — to move! Speak to the mountain, and it will obey you!

Jesus was telling His disciples that there is power in words. He was teaching them about faith in God. When Jesus said, "Have faith in God" (v. 22), He was saying, "Have faith in God, and have faith in the faith that's been put within you!"

Jesus said in Mark 11:24, *"Therefore I say unto you, What things soever ye desire, when ye pray, believe that ye receive them, and ye shall have them."* He was saying that when you go before the Father in prayer, believe that you have what you desire and pray for as soon as you pray.

You don't have to go to God, asking repeatedly, "Please, Lord, *please!* Do this for me." No, He is your Daddy. He hears you the first time you ask. God isn't dull of hearing. So when you pray, say, "Thank

You, Father. I believe I receive it." And if you believe you receive it, then act like it's so — talk like it's so, walk like it's so, and shout the victory like it's so! Go to bed and get up praising God, and do it every day, because you know it's so! This is the law of faith — you believe, and, therefore, you speak (*see* Second Corinthians 4:13).

Pray, Believe, Receive, and *Forgive*

Now there is another part to this law of faith. In Mark 11:24, Jesus said, *"Therefore I say unto you, What things soever ye desire, when ye pray, believe that ye receive them, and ye shall have them."* But notice there's an "and" that comes after that, in verse 25.

> **MARK 11:25,26**
> **25 AND when ye stand praying, FORGIVE, if ye have ought against any: that your Father also which is in heaven may forgive you your trespasses.**
> **26 But if ye do not forgive, neither will your Father which is in heaven forgive your trespasses.**

The law of faith is not just believing and saying; the law of faith is believing, saying, and *forgiving. Forgiveness is part of the law of faith!* In fact, you are not operating in faith if you're not operating in forgiveness. In Mark 11:25, forgiveness is connected to the previous verse, verse 24, the verse about faith. If you can't let go of the problem you have with someone, then you can't receive from God. If you can't let go of how you feel about a person — if you can't forgive him — you will not be able to receive anything from God.

This is something Jesus emphasized in His last week on the earth. Therefore, we must pay particular attention to what He was saying.

Chapter 3

Seedtime and Harvest: God's Plan for the Recipients Of the Earth

During the last few hours before Jesus sits down for the Last Supper with His disciples, Jesus begins to speak in parables.

In Mark chapter 11, Jesus taught on the law of faith, which includes forgiveness. But in Mark chapter 12, Jesus begins to speak in parables. This takes place in the wake of Judas selling out Jesus for thirty pieces of silver, the crowd saying, "Crucify Him," and Jesus hanging on the Cross, saying, "My God, why have You forsaken Me?" During His last remaining hours, Jesus shares some final words.

> **MARK 12:1**
> 1 And he [Jesus] **began to speak unto them by parables. A certain man planted a vineyard, and set an hedge about it, and digged a place for the winefat, and built a tower, and let** [leased] **it out to husbandmen, and went into a far country.**

The vineyard Jesus is talking about is the earth. God rented out the vineyard. Renting is leasing. God leased out the earth. When did He do that?

When God made Adam. Remember what God told Adam in the Book of Genesis.

GENESIS 1:26-28
26 And God said, Let us make man in our image, after our likeness: AND LET THEM HAVE DOMINION over the fish of the sea, and over the fowl of the air, and over the cattle, and over all the earth, and over every creeping thing that creepeth upon the earth.
27 So God created man in his own image, in the image of God created he him; male and female created he them.
28 And God blessed them, and God said unto them, Be fruitful, and multiply, and replenish the earth, and subdue it: and have dominion over the fish of the sea, and over the fowl of the air, and over every living thing that moveth upon the earth.

God made Adam the "god" of this world. He leased the earth out to him.

Now a lease doesn't mean that you have permanent possession. There is a time when the lease runs out, and the property returns to the rightful owner. Mark 12:1 says, *"...A certain man planted a vineyard, and set an hedge about it, and digged a place for the winefat, and built a tower, and let it out to husbandmen* [God leased it out to mankind]*, and went into a far country."*

Adam Turns Over the Lease to Satan

Now remember, Adam sinned in the Garden of Eden. Second Corinthians 4:4 says, *"In whom the god of this world hath blinded the minds of them which believe not, lest the light of the glorious gospel of Christ, who is the image of God, should shine unto them."* Who is "the god of this world" in this verse? It's not Adam; it's Satan. Somehow Satan, who blinds the minds of people who don't know Jesus, became god of this world. When did that take place? In the Garden of Eden.

God had told Adam, "You can have everything in this Garden except the one tree in the middle" (Gen. 2:16,17). The Garden of Eden stretched from Saudi Arabia to Central Africa. There were thousands of miles of every kind of fruit tree, plant, and anything Adam could desire. God met his needs physically, mentally, and even socially — He gave him a woman to love him and help him. God gave Adam everything he wanted and said, "All this is yours except the one tree in the middle."

Of course, you know what Adam did. Actually, he and his wife both disobeyed God. They obeyed Satan, and Satan then became the god of this world. As long as Adam and Eve obeyed God, things worked for them and for God; His plan was being accomplished. But when they obeyed Satan, things worked *against* them and *for* Satan. And Adam and his wife Eve became slaves in the slave market of sin.

Thank God, this deal was only a lease and not a complete sale! If it had been a complete sale, there would be no hope for us at all. But Jesus came to help us while the lease was still in effect. He came to set us free from that tyrant Satan and to bring back what He intended for Adam in the first place.

Jesus Restores the Lease

God told Adam, in effect, "As long as you have this lease, you have dominion over everything in the planet. You have dominion over everything that flies, walks, swims, or crawls. You're the man! You're in charge; whatever you say is what will come to pass." Man lost that dominion when he sinned, but through His death, burial, and resurrection, Jesus restored that dominion to you and me.

Let's continue with this parable in Mark chapter 12.

MARK 12:2-4
2 And at the season he sent to the husbandmen a servant, that he might receive from the husbandmen of the fruit of the vineyard.
3 And they caught him, and beat him, and sent him away empty.

4 And again he sent unto them another servant; and at him they cast stones, and wounded him in the head, and sent him away shamefully handled.

According to this parable, God kept sending servants to His vineyard. Now before Jesus came to the earth, the servants that the Lord sent were the prophets. He sent the prophets to preach the Word of God. And since the prophets preached the Word of God, we know God intended for men to hear that Word, repent of their sins, bow their knees to Him, and become servants of God Almighty. God expected to reap a return from the lease He let out.

But this passage says they (the husbandmen or "tenants") beat those prophets and killed them. This happened to prophet after prophet. Satan understood that those prophets were handling the Word of God. So he decided to get rid of them, and he used man to do it.

MARK 12:5-9

5 And again he [God] sent another [servant]; and him they killed, and many others; beating some, and killing some.

6 Having yet therefore one son, his wellbeloved, he sent him also last unto them, saying, They will reverence my son.

7 But those husbandmen said among themselves, This is the heir; come, let us kill him, and the inheritance shall be ours.

8 And they took him, and killed him, and cast him out of the vineyard.
9 What shall therefore the lord of the vineyard do? he will come and destroy the husbandmen, and will give the vineyard unto others.

Notice verse 7: *"But those husbandmen said among themselves, This is the heir; come, let us kill him, and the inheritance shall be ours."* In other words, Satan said in verse 7, "The Son has come. If we kill Him, we get everything forever."

There was a first group of husbandmen — the chosen ones, the Jewish people under the Old Covenant — that God wanted to get His salvation to. So God sent His Son, Jesus, to see that they be restored.

But who are the "others" mentioned in verse 9 who would get the opportunity to receive eternal salvation? It's you and me, the Gentiles who didn't even know God. The Gospel was sent to you and me who weren't the chosen people. God sent the Apostle Paul to bring the Gospel to us, to give us the opportunity to get in on the blessings of God and His plan for the earth.

New Recipients of the Earth Lease

You can't work for or earn something that is given to you as a gift. The only thing you can do with something *given* to you is just *receive* it. The salvation offered by Jesus does not come by your good works. You're not saved because you give money to the poor or because you don't smoke, drink, steal, commit adultery — or because you think you're better than somebody else!

You don't have the power to wash away the sin that came upon mankind. But God sent One who was sinless. God said, "I'm going to give My Son, My only begotten Son. And He will carry your sin. All you have to do is receive the gift of salvation offered to you through Him." John 3:16 says, *"For God so loved the world, that he gave his only begotten Son. . . ."* Thank God for the Gift!

God said, "I will give the earth to anyone who will believe, anyone who will receive the Son. The earth will belong to him." When they speak to a tree, it has to act. When they tell mountains to move, the mountains have to move. When they speak to anything on the planet and believe, it will come to pass, because they are the recipients of the earth lease.

I'm glad God didn't give up on us. After Adam disobeyed, God could have said, "This is My planet, and I'll just wait until the lease is up. Let them die. I'll start all over again with another group." He could have left us in this destroyed earth with nothing but sin, sickness, poverty, degradation, fear, and depression. We would have no way out — no hope! But God loved us so much that He sent His Son Jesus.

A New Creation and a New Plan

As I said, God could have left the earth the way it was — steeped in sin — until the lease ran out whereby He could have taken it back and cleaned it up again. In a sense, that's what He did the first time. Genesis 1:1 and 2 says, ". . . *God created the heaven and the earth. And the earth was without form, and void. . . .*" The place was destroyed. How do I know that? Because when God creates something, it is not without form and void!

You see, there was a battle between Satan and one third of the angels and God and the other two thirds of the angels. The Bible tells us that Satan lost. He was thrown out of Heaven. Jesus said, "I saw Satan fall like lightning to the ground" (Luke 10:18). When Satan hit this planet, he destroyed everything (*see* John 10:10).

There was a civilization here before the re-creation of the earth. Remember what God told Adam and Eve in the Garden of Eden. He said, "Multiply and *replenish* the earth" (Gen. 1:28). What does "replenish" mean? The word replenish means to *restock*.

There were dinosaurs on the earth at one time, and there were many other things as well. But they were wiped out when Satan came and destroyed everything. So God said, "Wait a minute! Let Me re-create this thing." He said, "Light be!" And light was! So He re-created the planet. Then He created a lease and gave it to Adam, telling him to do with the earth what he wanted. Satan got back at God by getting to Adam. But God said, "I'm not quitting."

Remember, God never loses! And if you stay with God and trust Him, you aren't going to lose, either. Romans 8:37 says, *"Nay, in all these things we are MORE THAN CONQUERORS THROUGH HIM that loved us."* First John 5:4 and 5 says, *". . . this is the victory that overcometh the world, even our faith. Who is he that overcometh the world, but he that believeth that Jesus is the Son of God?"*

You are an overcomer! You are a winner — even if you don't feel like one, even if you don't look like one, even if others say you aren't one! You need to say what *God* says about you!

How the Word of God Changed the Earth

Earlier in this chapter, we read in Mark chapter 12 about prophets whom God sent to preach the Word of God. The Bible says that the Word of God is like rain from Heaven: It falls to the earth and waters the earth so that it will bring forth and bud (Isa. 55:10,11). These prophets spoke the Word of God in the earth, and it started changing the hearts of men, turning them from Adam's way to God's way.

God spoke through these prophets, proclaiming that the Son was coming. "His Name will be called Wonderful, Counselor, The Mighty God, The Everlasting Father, The Prince of Peace. And of His Kingdom, there will be no end. He will be born of a virgin. And that holy thing that comes out of her womb will be called the Son of God. He will be called Immanuel, meaning *God with us*" (Isa. 9:6; 7:14).

God spoke these things through the mouth of a man. And Satan killed that prophet. God kept sending prophets until, finally, the season came. God said, "I'm going to send My Son now, My only beloved Son, because I lost My family when they went over to the devil. But I'm going to get My family back!" (God took back what was stolen from Him. And because you're His child, God expects you to act like He did. You can get back whatever the devil has stolen from *you*!)

So Jesus came to the earth. And Satan said, "Kill Him! Kill the Son, and we get to have it all." At first, Satan didn't understand. He didn't understand how Jesus came in the first place.

Remember, when Jesus came up against evil spirits, they would say, "We know who you are. You're the Holy One of God. You can't torment us before the time [before the lease runs out]." (*See* Matthew 8:29.) Man — Adam — gave Satan the lease, and only man could take it back. That's why Jesus had to come to the earth legally, as a man. He couldn't come as God and take back for Adam what Adam forfeited. Jesus had to come as a man.

Those evil spirits didn't understand that Jesus hadn't come to the earth as God. He came here legally — as a man. So when Satan and his cohorts came against Jesus, He had legal authority. He had a legal right to be there. When those spirits cried out, "...*What have we to do with thee, Jesus, thou Son of God? art thou come hither to torment us before the time?*" (Matt. 8:29), Jesus said, "Come out." He cast them out, because, unlike Adam, Satan had no authority over Jesus for one simple reason: Jesus was without sin.

Every man born after Adam was born with the nature of death in him. Death is passed from the father unto the child, but Jesus was born of a virgin. He is the Second Adam (1 Cor. 15:45). And because He had no sin, Satan had no authority over Him. You see, Satan was only able to gain dominance over the first Adam through an act of Adam's own will. He couldn't just grab Adam, throw him down, and take him over! No, Adam and Eve had to obey him, and they did. They submitted themselves to him and sinned.

Jesus is the Heir in Mark chapter 12. All things belong to Him. He made all things, and, ultimately, they belong to Him (John 1:3,10). But Jesus doesn't want them by Himself. He wants His brothers and sisters to be with Him. So during the last few days of Jesus' time on earth, He explained what was happening. He explained what He was doing here on the earth. He did this so that the time would come when you and I would understand our place in Him by the revelation of the Holy Ghost. (I will talk about this in more detail later in the book.)

Seedtime and Harvest

Everything in the earth exists as a result of seedtime and harvest. Even the salvation God provided for mankind came as a result of a seed. God sent His Son as a seed into the earth to redeem us.

John chapter 12 describes how seedtime and harvest works.

JOHN 12:24
24 Verily, verily, I say unto you, Except a corn of wheat fall into the ground and die, it abideth alone: but if it die, it bringeth forth much fruit.

God is the author of seedtime and harvest. Seedtime and harvest is not something related to money; it is the method by which everything works. Everything in the earth is the result of seedtime and harvest.

You are the result of seedtime and harvest. Your father carried you in his body. You were a seed swimming in the body of your father, and you were planted in the fertile ground of your mother. After nine months, you came forth and were born. Now you are here today planting seeds and producing a harvest.

Everything in the earth works this way. That is why abortion is wrong. It violates the principle of seedtime and harvest. It goes against the laws God set in motion in the earth in Genesis chapter 8.

So since God wanted His children back, what did He have to do? He had to follow the laws He set up for the whole universe. He had to operate the law of seedtime and harvest. He had to sow His best seed to get the full harvest He wanted. He started out with the seed of the spoken word and ended up with the Living Seed, Jesus.

How You Can Bear Much Fruit

Jesus said, "Except the corn of wheat falls to the ground and dies, it abides alone" (John 12:24). You can take a seed and put it somewhere, but it won't become anything more unless it is planted. This is true in every area of your life.

The Bible says, *"Give, and it shall be given unto you . . ."* (Luke 6:38). If you want love, you have to give love. You have to give your best love in order to get back a lot of love. You have to help someone else have joy so that joy can come to you. If you want a financial harvest, you have to give money.

God had a need: to get you and me back. And God gave out of His need. You are important in the eyes of God. You are the most important thing in the universe to God. When you curse another man, you are cursing God's creation. It is wrong; it is sin. It violates God's system.

Let's continue reading in John chapter 12 regarding seedtime and harvest.

JOHN 12:25
25 He that loveth his life shall lose it; and he that hateth his life in this world shall keep it unto life eternal.

Jesus said, "He that loves his life shall lose it." If you love your life so much that you try to hold onto it, you will lose it. Selfishness is nothing but fear of not getting what you want. Fear produces selfishness. You hold on to your love because you're afraid that if you love somebody else, you're going to get hurt and it's not going to come back to you. You hold on to forgiveness and won't forgive a person, because you are concerned that forgiveness won't be offered to you in the same way. You hold on to your money, thinking, *I have to keep what I have so I won't lose it*. But it doesn't work like that. Whatever you hold onto, you will lose.

God's entire system is about loving others. It's about giving to others; it produces a cycle. With God, everything is connected to something else. Whether you like it or not, you are connected to black folks, white folks, yellow folks, and red folks. Now Satan does everything he can to interrupt God's system, to cut us off. He tries to get us out of the flow of giving in every area of our lives.

Have you ever heard the saying, "Whatever goes around comes around"? Remember, as a man sows, he will also reap (Gal. 6:7). As a man gives in a good measure, it will come back to him in a good measure, "pressed down, shaken together, and running over" (Luke 6:38). That's the way it works.

There is a negative side to this system as well. If you give hate, you will get hate. If you give fear, then fear is coming back to you.

Jesus says, *"He that loveth his life shall lose it; and he that hateth his life in this world shall keep it unto life eternal"* (John 12:25). In order to win in life, you must be willing to give your life in this earth to Jesus. If you just focus on this life and forget about God and what He wants you to do on the earth, you will do what *you* want. You will eat, drink, and be merry. But God said that if you want the big prize (and the big prize is that you never die — you live eternally), you must plant your life and receive from the One who planted His life first — Jesus.

It isn't a waste when you give into the Kingdom of God. It's not a waste when you serve in the Kingdom of God. It's not a waste of your time if you go to church two, three, or four times a week. You are giving your life and sowing toward a prize. And billions of years from now while others are in hell in eternal death, you will be in the very Presence of God.

Let God Honor You

Let's continue reading in John chapter 12.

JOHN 12:26
**26 If any man serve me [Jesus], let him follow me;
and where I am, there shall also my servant be: if
any man serve me, him will my Father honour.**

Having the Father honor you is the greatest
thing that could ever happen to you. When God
honors you, He exalts you in due time (1 Peter 5:6).
When God honors you, He calls you to win in every
way. He makes your enemies to be at peace with you
(Prov. 16:7). He prepares a table before you in the
presence of your enemies (Ps. 23:5).

When you are someone who serves God, the
Lord becomes your Shepherd, and you have no
wants. He makes you to rest in blessed, green,
prosperous pastures. He leads you beside water
that is crystal clear when everybody else is in
drought (Ps. 23:2).

Life Under the *S-o-n*

Let's look briefly at the Twenty-Third Psalm.

PSALM 23:1-6
1 The Lord is my shepherd; I shall not want.

2 He maketh me to lie down in green pastures: he
leadeth me beside the still waters.
3 He restoreth my soul: he leadeth me in the paths
of righteousness for his name's sake.
4 Yea, though I walk through the valley of the
shadow of death, I will fear no evil: for thou art
with me; thy rod and thy staff they comfort me.
5 Thou preparest a table before me in the presence
of mine enemies: thou anointest my head with oil;
my cup runneth over.
6 Surely goodness and mercy shall follow me all
the days of my life: and I will dwell in the house of
the Lord for ever.

I tell you, Psalm 23 is not about Heaven. Psalm
23 is about earth under the *S-o-n*! This is what we
have through Jesus — this is ours as a result of the
Seed.

Look at verse 3: *"He restoreth my soul...."* When
Adam sinned, his soul was destroyed. The first
thing that came out of his mouth was, "I'm afraid"
(Gen. 3:10). But when you serve God, fear is no
longer a part of your consciousness. Worry and
doubt can't stay. You're free. What peace you have
because you serve Him!

Verse 4 says, *"Yea, though I walk through the
valley of the shadow of death, I will fear no evil: for
thou art with...."* I like that word "through,"
because it means you go in on one side, but you
come out on the other! In other words, you don't

camp in the valley — you go *through* it! You might be in the valley now, but you can confidently say, "Watch me, Devil, I'm going through the valley of the shadow of death. And while I'm going, I will fear no evil because the Lord is with me. His rod and His staff comfort me. And He prepares for me a table of blessings right in the face of my enemies." (You know Psalm 23 isn't talking about Heaven, because we won't have any enemies in Heaven.)

Psalm 23:5 says, *"Thou preparest a table before me in the presence of mine enemies: thou anointest my head with oil; my cup runneth over."* God is spreading out a table to those who will receive the free gift of Jesus. It's a table of healing, a table of right-standing, a table of prosperity, a table of righteousness, peace, and joy in the Holy Ghost (Rom. 14:17)! That table is a table of love, a table of strength, a table of never being bound again and of knowing that you're a winner. It's a table of anointing — of yoke-destroying, burden-removing power!

Friend, God has a table in front of you. So get a helping of healing! Whatever you need, it's there on the table!

Psalm 23:6 says, *"Surely goodness and mercy shall follow me all the days of my life: and I will dwell in the house of the Lord for ever."* But in order to receive all of this, you must give up your life. Jesus gave up His life, and He expects you to do the same, except He wants you to give up your life *to Him*. Give up your life and receive the blessings of God!

Chapter 4
Three Life Lessons

During the last few days of Jesus' ministry on the earth, He shared some vitally important truths that He wanted us to get hold of so we could practice them in our lives. Remember that a teacher usually finishes his teaching with the most important points — the points he wants you to remember most. Jesus was no different. He finished His time on earth sharing the most important things He wanted us to remember. In this chapter, we are continuing our study of Jesus' last hours before the Last Supper.

Life Lesson Number One:
Walk in love

Jesus taught about the most important commandment of all in the following passage.

MATTHEW 22:36-40
36   Master, which is the great commandment in the law?
37   Jesus said unto him, Thou shalt love the Lord thy God with all thy heart, and with all thy soul, and with all thy mind.
38   This is the first and great commandment.

> **39   And the second is like unto it, Thou shalt love thy neighbour as thyself.**
> **40   On these two commandments hang all the law and the prophets.**

Jesus called the commandment to love God the "first and great" commandment (v. 38). He also said that all the Law and the prophets hang on these two commandments: 1) *You are to love the Lord your God with everything you have, with your entire being*; and 2) *you are to love your neighbor as you love yourself.* Obviously, Jesus was assuming that you love yourself. You are to treat your neighbor as good as or better than you would treat yourself.

This is a lesson Jesus wanted us to remember, because He taught it right at the end of His life and ministry on the earth. He wanted us to walk in love. After He was hung on the Cross, He wanted us to remember what He said to us. And after He rose from the dead, He wanted us to remember this teaching to love God and others.

Life Lesson Number Two:
Be Faithful With What God Gives You

Let's look at what else Jesus taught in His last few hours, just before He had what we call the Last

Supper with His disciples and went to the Garden of Gethsemane.

> **MATTHEW 25:14,15**
> 14 For the kingdom of heaven is as a man travelling into a far country, who called his own servants, and delivered unto them his goods.
> 15 And unto one he gave five talents, to another two, and to another one; to every man according to his several ability; and straightway took his journey.

A talent was a unit of money and, back in those days, was worth $935. In these verses, Jesus was actually talking about money. But because what He taught is a principle in the Word of God, it can apply to other areas as well. In other words, it doesn't *just* apply to money; it applies to other things too. Verse 15 says that Jesus gave to each man according to his ability. Let's continue reading.

> **MATTHEW 25:16-20**
> 16 Then he that had received the five talents went and traded with the same, and made them other five talents.
> 17 And likewise he that had received two, he also gained other two.
> 18 But he that had received one went and digged in the earth, and hid his lord's money.
> 19 After a long time the lord of those servants cometh, and reckoneth with them.

20   And so he that had received five talents came
and brought other five talents, saying, Lord, thou
deliveredst unto me five talents: behold, I have
gained beside them five talents more.

What did the man with five talents do? He took
what his master had given to him — nearly $5,000 —
and invested it. Then he brought more to be used in
his master's service. God expects us to use what He
has given us for His service.

Let's see how the man's master replied to the
news.

MATTHEW 25:21- 23
21   His lord said unto him, WELL DONE, THOU
GOOD AND FAITHFUL SERVANT: thou hast been
faithful over a few things, I will make thee ruler
over many things: enter thou into the joy of thy
lord.
22   He also that had received two talents came
and said, Lord, thou deliveredst unto me two
talents: behold, I have gained two other talents
beside them.
23   His lord said unto him, Well done, good and
faithful servant; thou hast been faithful over a few
things, I will make thee ruler over many things:
enter thou into the joy of thy lord.

Look at verses 22 and 23. The same thing
happened with the man who'd been given two
talents. He also took what his master had given him

and invested it. He put the money back into the hands of the master, and the master said to him, "Well done, thou good and faithful servant."

Let's read what happened to the man who received one talent.

> MATTHEW 25:24-29
> 24 . . .he which had received the one talent came and said, Lord, I knew thee that thou art an hard man, reaping where thou hast not sown, and gathering where thou hast not strawed:
> 25 And I was afraid, and went and hid thy talent in the earth: lo, there thou hast that is thine.
> 26 His lord answered and said unto him, THOU WICKED AND SLOTHFUL SERVANT, thou knewest that I reap where I sowed not, and gather where I have not strawed:
> 27 Thou oughtest therefore to have put my money to the exchangers, and then at my coming I should have received mine own with usury.
> 28 Take therefore the talent from him, and give it unto him which hath ten talents.
> 29 For unto every one that hath shall be given, and he shall have abundance: but from him that hath not shall be taken away even that which he hath.

We know that when the master is mentioned in this parable, it is referring to God. Let me paraphrase what this servant was thinking when he failed to invest his one talent. He thought, *Lord, You're not doing anything; I'm the one doing everything. I'm the one who works hard for my money. I'm the one who has done all the production. This doesn't belong to You.*

Notice that this man who didn't do what God told him to do didn't get anymore. In fact, what he had was taken away from him and given to the servant with the ten talents (v. 28). Verse 30 says, *"And cast ye the unprofitable servant into outer darkness: there shall be weeping and gnashing of teeth."* But the other two men who used what God had given them — who did what God told them to do with it — got more!

Life Lesson Number Three: Help Those in Need

We've read, sermonized, and heard much about the following passage of Scripture concerning "sheep and goats." But I want you to read it closely, because these words were among the last that Jesus shared on the earth before His crucifixion.

> MATTHEW 25:31-40
> 31 When the Son of man shall come in his glory, and all the holy angels with him, then shall he sit upon the throne of his glory:
> 32 And before him shall be gathered all nations: and he shall separate them one from another, as a shepherd divideth his sheep from the goats:

33 And he shall set the sheep on his right hand, but the goats on the left.

34 Then shall the King say unto them on his right hand, Come, ye blessed of my Father, inherit the kingdom prepared for you from the foundation of the world:

35 For I was an hungred, and ye gave me meat: I was thirsty, and ye gave me drink: I was a stranger, and ye took me in:

36 Naked, and ye clothed me: I was sick, and ye visited me: I was in prison, and ye came unto me.

37 Then shall the righteous answer him, saying, Lord, when saw we thee an hungred, and fed thee? or thirsty, and gave thee drink?

38 When saw we thee a stranger, and took thee in? or naked, and clothed thee?

39 Or when saw we thee sick, or in prison, and came unto thee?

40 And the King shall answer and say unto them, Verily I say unto you, Inasmuch as ye have done it unto one of the least of these my brethren, ye have done it unto me.

In verses 35 and 36, when Jesus referred to Himself as hungry, thirsty, a stranger, naked, sick, and imprisoned, He was talking about individuals. He was identifying with individual people, namely the "down and out," because He said in verse 40, "... *Inasmuch as ye have done it unto one of the least of these my brethren, ye have done it unto me.*"

Jesus was talking about those who were bound — about those who were destitute, sick, and incarcerated. And He was addressing us as individuals, not just as a corporate body. He wanted us to visit the imprisoned and sick. Jesus wanted to make sure that we would assist people who needed assistance. He was leaving us this reminder in His last few hours on the earth.

Chapter 5
The Last Promises of Jesus

In the last chapter, we looked briefly at three things Jesus wanted us to do: 1) *Walk in love*; 2) *be faithful with what God gives us*; and 3) *help those in need.* What else did Jesus want us to know in His last hours on the earth?

I want to look at three chapters in the Book of John — 14, 15, and 16 — at some of the promises of Jesus as well as some lessons He wanted us to learn about faith, prayer, and the ministry of the Holy Spirit.

A Place Prepared for You

In the following passage in John chapter 14, Jesus tells His disciples that when He goes, He will be involved in preparing a place for them in Heaven. He was not only talking to His disciples — He was talking to you and me too. Let's read what Jesus said.

> **JOHN 14:1-4**
> **1 Let not your heart be troubled: ye believe in God, believe also in me.**

2 In my Father's house are many mansions: if it were not so, I would have told you. I go to prepare a place for you.

3 And if I go and prepare a place for you, I will come again, and receive you unto myself; that where I am, there ye may be also.

4 And whither I go ye know, and the way ye know.

The day is coming when we are going to be with Jesus, so He is in the process of preparing a house for you and for me. Now the house that Jesus is preparing for you is the finest thing you could ever imagine. It can't even be compared to the most magnificent house you can find in a magazine. God is preparing the best for His children.

Anybody who knows the Lord and has gone on to be with the Lord is in his or her mansion right now. There are many people who never had a mansion on earth. But if you live here on this earth for a hundred years, that will be a very short time compared to all of eternity. In Heaven, you will have the finest mansion in all the universe, and it will be yours forever.

God loves you so much. He has set aside a special place for you in Heaven. Jesus said it Himself: "I go to prepare a place for you."

You Can Walk in God's Power

Further on in John 14, Jesus continues speaking about His departure and what would happen as a result of His going to the Father.

> **JOHN 14:12**
> 12 Verily, verily, I say unto you, He that believeth on me, the works that I do shall he do also; and greater works than these shall he do; because I go unto my Father.

In other words, Jesus was saying, "I'm getting out of the way so you can do even better stuff than what I did on earth." Jesus was saying that you can walk in God's power because "I go unto My Father."

'Ask the Father in My Name'

Then notice what Jesus said right after that.

> **JOHN 14:13,14**
> 13 And whatsoever ye shall ask in my name, that will I do, that the Father may be glorified in the Son.
> 14 If ye shall ask any thing in my name, I will do it.

Jesus was letting everyone know that He was going to leave, but that He was also going to leave us with whatever we needed. He left us His Name to use in prayer and told us that whatever we needed, we,too, could ask of the Father and it would be done for us. He said, "Whatsoever you shall ask in My Name, that will I do." Then He said it again: "If you shall ask anything in My Name, I will do it"!

This is one of the last promises Jesus makes before He leaves the earth. (I don't know about you, but I believe that whatever Jesus says is so!) He taught us to pray to the Father, not "for Jesus' sake," but "in Jesus' Name." The Name of Jesus is the key that "unlocks" Heaven.

Another Comforter

Continuing in John chapter 14, we read what Jesus promised concerning "another Comforter" — the Holy Spirit — whom Jesus said would abide with us forever.

> **JOHN 14:16-18**
> **16 And I [Jesus] will pray the Father, and he shall give you ANOTHER COMFORTER, that he may abide with you for ever;**
> **17 Even the Spirit of truth; whom the world cannot receive, because it seeth him not, neither knoweth him: but ye know him; for he dwelleth with you, and shall be in you.**
> **18 I will not leave you comfortless: I will come to you.**

In John chapter 14, Jesus was letting His disciples know that He was about to be crucified. He was about to leave this planet. But He said that He would not leave them by themselves. He was going to leave them with another Comforter, whom Jesus also referred to as the Spirit of Truth (v. 17).

In addition to giving us the Name of Jesus to use, Jesus also gave us the Holy Spirit — the Comforter, the Spirit of Truth — who teaches us all things and brings all things to our remembrance.

JOHN 14:26
26 But the Comforter, which is the Holy Ghost, whom the Father will send in my name, he shall teach you all things, and bring all things to your remembrance, whatsoever I have said unto you.

What things would the Holy Spirit bring back to our remembrance? This verse tells us: "...*whatsoever I* [Jesus] *have said unto you.*" In other words, Jesus was saying, "All of this teaching I have given you, the Holy Spirit will bring back to your remembrance when you need it." Not only that, but Jesus said He would teach us "all things." How much is left after "*all*"? Jesus was saying, in effect, "The Holy Spirit will teach you whatever you need to know to win in life while I'm gone."

Now if Jesus taught you how to do something, that means you can do it! Philippians 4:13 says, "I can do all things through Christ who strengthens me." The word "Christ" means *Anointed One*. It is through His anointing that you can do *all* things! The anointing — the Holy Spirit, the Comforter — is inside you. So never say you can't do something that the Bible says you can do. Look to the Holy Spirit within for help.

What else did Jesus say about the coming of the Holy Spirit? Let's read in John chapter 16.

> **JOHN 16:7-11**
> **7 Nevertheless I tell you the truth; It is expedient for you that I go away: for if I go not away, the Comforter will not come unto you; but if I depart, I will send him unto you.**
> **8 And when he is come, he will reprove the world of sin, and of righteousness, and of judgment:**
> **9 Of sin, because they believe not on me;**
> **10 Of righteousness, because I go to my Father, and ye see me no more;**
> **11 Of judgment, because the prince of this world is judged.**

Who is "the prince of this world" in verse 11? The prince of this world is Satan. Jesus said, "When I leave, the Holy Spirit will come, and the prince of this world will be judged!" Judged how? From this perspective: His power will be broken, and he will be defeated.

What was about to happen on that Cross was the beginning of the end for the devil. First Corinthians 2:7 and 8 says, *"But we speak the wisdom of God in a mystery, even the hidden wisdom, which God ordained before the world unto our glory: Which none of the princes of this world knew: for had they known it, they would not have crucified the Lord of glory."*

The crucifixion of Jesus Christ would break Satan's grip over his slaves, which were you and me. Jesus said that the prince of the world would be judged; he would be rendered guilty! And all of those who were under his grip would be set free!

Let's continue reading about what Jesus said concerning the ministry of the Holy Spirit.

> **JOHN 16:12,13**
> **12 I have yet many things to say unto you, but ye cannot bear them now.**
> **13 Howbeit when he, the Spirit of truth, is come, he will guide you into all truth: for he shall not speak of himself; but whatsoever he shall hear, that shall he speak: and he will shew you things to come.**

The Holy Spirit will show you things to come; He will announce to you what is coming. It says, "He shall not speak of Himself, but whatsoever He shall hear, He will speak, and He will show you the future."

The Holy Spirit will always give you "inside information" in advance if you will listen to Him. You never have to be caught by surprise in your life ever again. If you spend time with the Comforter, He will reveal to you *what's* coming and *how* it's coming. For example, He will tell you and get you ready for what the devil has in mind for you so that you can always ambush the devil's ambush!

It was not the end when Jesus died. God was working out His plan of redemption, and with that plan, He sent us the Holy Spirit. Thank God for the ministry of the Holy Spirit and for these last teachings of Jesus!

God Wants More From You!

In a previous chapter, I talked briefly about how you can bear much fruit for God by planting a seed. But there is more to reaping than just sowing or planting. God wants us to clean ourselves up and overcome weaknesses in the flesh so that we can produce good things for His glory.

> **JOHN 15:1-3**
> **1** I [Jesus] **am the true vine, and my Father is the husbandman.**

2 Every branch in me that beareth not fruit he taketh away: and every branch that beareth fruit, he purgeth it, that it may bring forth more fruit.
3 Now ye are clean through the word which I have spoken unto you.

You are washed, cleaned, and made pure through the Word. The Psalmist wrote in Psalm 119:9, *"Wherewithal shall a young man cleanse his way? by taking heed thereto according to thy word."* The Word is what cleans you up!

If you seem to be weak in your flesh or in any way, then your problem is a Word shortage. If you keep putting the Word of God in you, filling yourself up with that Word, the Word will stop you from doing things you really don't want to do. The Word of God is full of power. The Word is full of "stoppability"! It can stop you from doing what you don't want to do. The Word will also cause you to do the things you should do. It is the strength you need at all times.

Abide in the Word

Let's continue reading in John chapter 15.

JOHN 15:4
4 Abide in me [Jesus], and I in you. As the branch cannot bear fruit of itself, except it abide in the vine; no more can ye, except ye abide in me.

Jesus said that the only way you are going to produce fruit is to get more of Him in you. The Greek word for "remain" means to *live in, settle down in, take up residence in,* and it implies *permanence.*

JOHN 15:7
7 If ye abide [remain] **in me, and my words abide in you, ye shall ask what ye will, and it shall be done unto you.**

If you continually live in, settle down in, take up residence in Jesus and His words, you shall ask what you will and it shall be done unto you! Was Jesus out of His mind when He said this? No! If you're abiding in the Word, and the Word is abiding — living, settling down, and taking up residence — in you, whatever you ask for according to that Word will be done for you.

But notice the "abiding" part of the contract. You see, if the Word of God is on the inside of you, you won't be asking God for four husbands or three wives; you won't be asking God for things that aren't scriptural. When the Word of God gets in you, it cleans you up. It enables you to ask aright, in faith and in line with the Word. And God will do it for you!

How is God glorified? Jesus told us just before He hung on that Cross: *"Herein is my Father glorified, that ye bear much fruit; so shall ye be my disciples"* (John 15:8).

God doesn't expect us to sit down and not produce while we are on this earth. He expects us to bear fruit and to have fullness of joy.

> **JOHN 15:10,11**
> **10 If ye keep my [Jesus] commandments, ye shall abide in my love; even as I have kept my Father's commandments, and abide in his love.**
> **11 These things have I spoken unto you, that my joy might remain in you, and that your joy might be full.**

Jesus said, "If you obey My commands, you will remain in My love, just as I have obeyed My Father's commands and remain in His love. I have told you this so that My joy may be in you and that your joy may be complete." The joy was gone from Jesus' disciples because they thought it was all going to be over when He hung on that tree. They were preparing to hide inside a room and wait for death to come get them too. They thought that once Jesus was killed, the Jews would be coming for them.

Jesus responded to their concerns by saying, *"This is my commandment, That ye love one another, as I have loved you. Greater love hath no man than this, that a man lay down his life for his friends"* (John 15:12,13).

We are getting closer to Jesus' last moments on the earth. We will see in the next chapter what Jesus shared with His disciples at the Last Supper and on the Mount of Olives.

Chapter 6
The Heart of a Servant

In Jesus' life and ministry, we see the heart of a servant. Wherever He went and whatever He did, He lived a lifestyle of servanthood. Jesus said that He came to this earth not to *be* served, but to serve (Matt. 20:28). And as the time of Jesus' life on earth comes to a close, we find much of His teaching focusing on this aspect of servanthood.

The Last Supper

The Last Supper was a real meal, but the way it has been depicted in many paintings is not accurate. There wasn't a beautiful, shiny table with all kinds of silverware. No, in that part of the world, people sat on the floor. They ate while sitting on the floor.

And Jesus didn't look like those Sunday school pictures, either. He didn't look like a Nordic ski man! No, Jesus was a Jew with Jewish features — a Jewish head and a Jewish nose. He was a rabbi sitting on the floor with His disciples, where they passed bread one to another. He was enjoying the last fellowship with His disciples while giving them the very last nuggets of teaching.

Let's read what happened at that table.

> **MATTHEW 26:20,26-28**
> **20 Now when the even was come, he sat down with the twelve. . . .**
> **26 And as they were eating, Jesus took bread, and blessed it, and brake it, and gave it to the disciples, and said, Take, eat; this is my body.**
> **27 And he took the cup, and gave thanks, and gave it to them, saying, Drink ye all of it;**
> **28 For this is my blood of the NEW TESTAMENT, which is shed for many for the remission of sins.**

Look at verse 28. Jesus said, "This is My blood of the New Testament." In other words, Jesus said, "A new covenant is coming. This cup represents the fact that I am in covenant with you, My followers."

Most of us don't understand the term "covenant." In the Old Testament, when the word covenant was used as an agreement between two parties, blood was usually spilled. They either pricked their thumbs or cut their wrists and then mingled the blood together. It was a blood covenant.

When Jesus told His disciples, "This cup is the new covenant in My blood," He was telling them that it was a blood covenant. In the Old Testament, if a man broke a blood covenant, that man had to die. But, you see, that word "covenant" is so strong that a man didn't dare break a blood covenant. When he gave his word, he would die for that word.

Jesus was saying, "I am entering into a blood covenant with you. This covenant shall never be broken. This cup represents something that is about to happen in a few hours. My blood is about to be shed, and when it's shed, it will represent my covenant with you — a covenant that I will never break."

Jesus was saying, "I would have to cease existing for this covenant to be broken. This cup is a symbolic reminder of the shedding of My blood and of all the things that will come about as a result of My blood."

So sitting on that dirt floor, those disciples drank from the cup that symbolized what was about to take place. Then after they sang a hymn, they went out to the Mount of Olives (Matt. 26:30).

'Will a Man Rob God?'

Let's read Luke's account of the events preluding the Last Supper.

LUKE 22:1-8
1 Now the feast of unleavened bread drew nigh, which is called the Passover.

2 And the chief priests and scribes sought how they
might kill him; for they feared the people.
3 Then entered Satan into Judas surnamed
Iscariot, being of the number of the twelve.
4 And he went his way, and communed with the
chief priests and captains, how he might betray
him unto them.
5 And they were glad, and covenanted to give him
money.
6 And he promised, and sought opportunity to
betray him unto them in the absence of the
multitude.
7 Then came the day of unleavened bread, when
the passover must be killed.
8 And he sent Peter and John, saying, Go and
prepare us the passover, that we may eat.

Here we see that they were about to begin the
Lord's Supper. Notice verse 3 says that Satan went
into Judas. How was it that Satan entered into
Judas? Well, if you read the other Gospels, you will
find that Judas' heart wasn't like the hearts of the
rest of the disciples. The rest of them made
mistakes, but they were honest at heart. But Judas
was not. Judas was stealing from God. Judas was
the treasurer, and he was stealing from the bag.

Now the Lord let Judas be the treasurer. Think
about that. What was God doing? He was giving
Judas an opportunity to go the right way, to go
against his tendencies. God will give you

opportunities. He will give you the chance to prove you can do it! But then, it's up to you.

Judas was stealing from the bag. The rest of the disciples didn't know he was doing it. But, of course, Jesus knew it by divine revelation. Anytime you steal from God or are dishonest, you open yourself up for Satan to gain entrance into your life. Remember what God told the people in Malachi?

> **MALACHI 3:8**
> **8 Will a man rob God? Yet ye have robbed me. But ye say, Wherein have we robbed thee? IN TITHES AND OFFERINGS.**

This is how Satan gets into your life — into your affairs, into your children's lives, into your family: when you decide to rob God and not give Him His due — the tithe and offerings.

Jesus the God-Man Exemplifies The Heart of a Servant

Now let's read John's account in John 13:2 through 5 of the events proceeding the Last Supper. We are down to the last hour of Jesus' teachings. Verse 1 of this passage says, *"Now before the feast of the passover, WHEN JESUS KNEW THAT HIS HOUR WAS COME THAT HE SHOULD DEPART*

OUT OF THIS WORLD UNTO THE FATHER, having loved his own which were in the world, he loved them unto the end." Jesus is-about to depart from this world and go to the Father.

JOHN 13:2-5
2 And supper being ended, the devil having now put into the heart of Judas Iscariot, Simon's son, to betray him;
3 Jesus knowing that the Father had given all things into his hands, and that he was come from God, and went to God;
4 He riseth from supper, and laid aside his garments; and took a towel, and girded himself.
5 After that he poureth water into a bason, and began to wash the disciples' feet, and to wipe them with the towel wherewith he was girded.

I want you to get this picture. Here is the Master of masters, the Creator of the universe, the One who along with the Father and the Holy Spirit made man. John 1:1 through 4 says, *"In the beginning was the Word, and the Word was with God, and the Word was God. . . . All things were made by him; and without him was not any thing made that was made. In him was life; and the life was the light of men."*

God wraps Himself in a towel and begins to take the part of a servant! Now realize, people didn't have shoes then like we have today. They had sandals. And they didn't have concrete; they walked on dirt and rocks. Plus their feet were dusty and dirty after sitting on a dirt floor.

Jesus pours water into the basin. Imagine the scenario. He takes the sandals off Thomas' feet and pours water on his feet as He begins to clean them. Then He goes to John and begins washing the dirt caked in the crevices of John's feet! He then cleans the feet of Philip and Matthew.

Then Jesus comes to Peter, and Peter says, "Lord, are You going to wash my feet?" (John 13:6). Jesus replied, "You do not realize now what I am doing, but later you will understand" (v. 7).

"No," Peter said, "You shall never wash my feet" (v. 8).

Peter, no doubt, was thinking, *What is this! I'm the servant; He's the Master. He's the One who has raised people from the dead. He's the One who has healed sicknesses of every kind. He's the One who changes people's lives in an instant. We are nothing — yet He is washing our feet? No, He isn't washing my feet!*

Peter's heart was right. He just didn't understand. Jesus answered Peter, saying, "Unless I wash you, you have no part with Me." (*See* John 13:4-8.)

Peter wasn't stupid. He answered Jesus, "Then, Lord, not just my feet, but my hands and my head as well!" (v. 9). In other words, Peter was saying, "I want to be with You even if I don't understand what's going on."

There might be times you don't understand what God is doing in your life, but submit to it anyway because He is teaching you something. He is developing you in some way. He is getting you ready for the ministry He has for you in the future.

Jesus had more to say along this line. Let's continue reading.

> **JOHN 13:10-14**
> **10 Jesus saith to him [Peter], He that is washed needeth not save to wash his feet, but is clean every whit: and ye are clean, but not all.**
> **11 For he knew who should betray him; therefore said he, Ye are not all clean.**
> **12 So after he had washed their feet, and had taken his garments, and was set down again, he said unto them, Know ye what I have done to you?**
> **13 Ye call me Master and Lord: and ye say well; for so I am.**
> **14 If I then, your Lord and Master, have washed your feet; ye also ought to wash one another's feet.**

What was Jesus teaching them? He was saying, "If I, being God, am not too good to get down in this dirt and take off your grubby sandals and wash between your toes, then *you* shouldn't have any trouble serving each other."

Are you too good to park cars? To work in the nursery? To work in children's church? To serve and help somebody else? The Lord said that you must be willing even to wash the congregation's feet.

We want to talk about receiving blessings, but there is a *blessing* side and a *love* side; there is a blessing side and a responsibility side. Both of them are important! We can't just love selective scriptures. We have to love all the scriptures.

Jesus set an example for us. We must bow down to one another, instead of fighting, arguing, and trying to get the best of each other. Jesus said that if we are willing to wash each other's feet, then we are all teammates; we're operating as a team. We're on the same side.

It doesn't matter who does what. It doesn't matter who takes the lead and who is seemingly behind the scenes. It doesn't matter whose name gets published and whose name doesn't. It doesn't matter because we are all on the same team, and we all wash each other's feet.

Jesus had yet more to say to His disciples concerning serving one another.

JOHN 13:15-17
15 For I have given you an example, that ye should do as I have done to you.
16 Verily, verily, I say unto you, The servant is not greater than his lord; neither he that is sent greater than he that sent him.
17 If ye know these things, happy are ye if ye do them.

There is joy when you serve others. That is what is wrong with some people. They don't have any joy, because they don't understand that everything in God's Kingdom is seedtime and harvest. You have to give of your yourself — of your money, your time, and your strength — in order to receive joy, peace, money, or anything else in the Kingdom. If you want to be happy, then help someone else be happy. Stop thinking selfishly about what you can get all the time.

Giving is the watchword of Christians and of Christianity. The Scripture says, *"For God so loved the world, that he GAVE his only begotten Son . . ."* (John 3:16). If Jesus taught us to serve one another and to give to one another, following His example, we should be doing these things too.

Chapter 7

What Jesus Taught About Prayer and Overcoming Temptation

After Jesus taught about serving one another, He went up to the Mount of Olives to pray. Luke 22:40 says, *"And when he [Jesus] was at the place, he said unto them, Pray that ye enter not into temptation."*

Jesus was teaching His disciples a lesson; He was telling them that prayer would keep them from falling.

Prayer is the key to not falling. If you have a flesh problem, a cold shower isn't what will keep you from falling! Having a relationship with God in prayer every day — spending time with Him in praise and worship and allowing the Holy Spirit to communicate with you — is what will keep you from falling. You will come to the place where you will fall in love with God; you will be more in love with God than with sin.

Prayer is what keeps you from lying, cheating, and stealing. Prayer is what keeps you from falling into *any* area of sin. If you don't have a prayer life, you will be vulnerable to the enemy.

It's not enough just to go to church and hear the Word. It's not enough to sing in the choir. You must have a personal relationship with God on a daily basis. The Lord wants you to "hang out" with Him.

The Strength of the Father Is Available for the Child

You and I are part of God's family. God is the Father, and you are the child. The Father wants to spend time with His child. And during the time the child spends with the Father, the strength of the Father gets into the child.

You see, you have to come to the place where when the enemy tempts you, you laugh at him. What God has for you is so much greater than that little crumb the devil has been trying to show you. The devil has been making you think that this is all you get — that if you don't take what he's offering, it's over; there won't be anything for you. But he is a liar and the father of lies (John 8:44).

God Has Blessings in Store for You!

What God has for you is so much better! He has a husband or wife for you, a job for you, healing for you — *blessing* for you! God opens the windows of Heaven for you and pours you out blessings you don't have room enough to receive (Mal. 3:10).

But you have to be patient. We are part of the "right now" generation. We want things instantly. But nothing in life worth having is obtained instantly. Everything is obtained by seedtime and harvest. So give the seed some time to work. Put in some time with that seed. Trust that the seed will work — that it will produce. If you do, you will get the full harvest. Don't pick the fruit off the tree when it is green. Wait until it's totally ripe.

Some people are anxious concerning the future. Even if they're being blessed today, they are unsure about the future. But time isn't your enemy; it's your friend. God can compress His blessing in you and make a year of blessing like a hundred! And He can do that for a hundred years and longer!

You will never lose when you follow God. When you do things God's way, the devil may tell you you're going to lose out, but you won't be losing a thing. You'll be gaining — on a long-term basis.

Be Committed to the Father's Will

Let's read what Jesus did on the Mount of Olives.

LUKE 22:40-42
40 And when he was at the place, he said unto them, Pray that ye enter not into temptation.
41 And he was withdrawn from them about a stone's cast, and kneeled down, and prayed,
42 Saying, Father, if thou be willing, remove this cup from me: NEVERTHELESS not my will, but thine, be done.

Oh, if only we would follow Jesus' example and say those words: "Not what I want Father — not what my dreams and desires are — but what *You* want"! How do you become that committed? By hanging out with God every day! The more you hang around somebody, the more you become like them.

Have you ever heard what is said about married people? It is said that when two people have been married to each other a long time, one person can start a sentence, and the other can finish it. The couple understands each other and knows exactly what the other person is going to say. Some people are married so long that they even begin to *look* like each other.

Whoever you hang out with rubs off on you. Second Corinthians 6:14 says, *"Be ye not unequally yoked together with unbelievers: for what fellowship hath righteousness with unrighteousness? and what communion hath light with darkness?"* But if you hang out with God Almighty, He will rub off on you! His Spirit will rub off on you, and you can't help but be what you need to be.

How To Deal With the Flesh

Let's continue reading about Jesus' prayer on the Mount of Olives.

> LUKE 22:43-46
> 43 And there appeared an angel unto him [Jesus] from heaven, strengthening him.
> 44 And being in an agony he prayed more earnestly: and his sweat was as it were great drops of blood falling down to the ground.
> 45 And when he rose up from prayer, and was come to his disciples, he found them sleeping for sorrow,
> 46 And said unto them, Why sleep ye? rise and pray, lest ye enter into temptation.

First, notice what Jesus did when His flesh was trying to push Him not to obey God's will. He *prayed.* You deal with the flesh through prayer and fellowship with God.

Let's look at verse 44. It says, *"And* [Jesus] *being in an agony he prayed more earnestly: and his sweat was as it were great drops of blood. . . ."* It didn't say His sweat *was* blood; it says it *was as if it were* blood. I mean, Jesus was facing a temptation. But He was praying and submitting Himself to God. He was hanging in there. And He was showing us how to deal with temptation and the flesh. What did He say in verse 46? He said, *". . . Why sleep ye? rise and pray, lest ye enter into temptation."* Jesus was telling the disciples, "You get up and pray lest you fail to do what you are supposed to do at this sacred time."

Peter's Test

Peter was one of the disciples whom Jesus told to pray and not to sleep. Let's read why Jesus said this.

> **LUKE 22:47-50**
> **47 And while he yet spake, behold a multitude, and he that was called Judas, one of the twelve, went before them, and drew near unto Jesus to kiss him.**
> **48 But Jesus said unto him, Judas, betrayest thou the Son of man with a kiss?**
> **49 When they** [the disciples] **which were about him saw what would follow, they said unto him, Lord, shall we smite with the sword?**
> **50 And one of them smote the servant of the high priest, and cut off his right ear.**

Verse 50 says that one of the disciples smote the high priest's servant with a sword. Can you guess which disciple? It was Peter. What did Jesus just get finished exhorting Peter about? About *praying*. He said to Peter, "*. . . Why sleep ye? rise and pray, lest ye enter into temptation*" (v. 46).

Jesus asked Peter why he was sleeping instead of praying. Jesus knew that Peter's test was coming up. Not only was this a test for Jesus in the Garden of Gethsemane, but it was also a test for His followers.

Now Peter's heart was right. But your heart can be right while your head is wrong! How do you reconcile your head and your heart? Through prayer!

Peter had taken out his sword and cut off that man's ear. I mean, Peter was ready to die! He had already told Jesus, "I'll die with You" (Matt. 26:35; Mark 14:31).

I like Peter. He meant business. None of the other disciples were saying anything when they came to seize Jesus. Their mouths were probably hanging open. Peter was the only one doing anything. It was the wrong thing, but at least he was doing something!

Peter chopped off the man's ear. His ear is lying on the ground, and he is no doubt screaming! Jesus answered, "No more of this!" (Luke 22:51). And He touched the man's ear and healed him.

That would have been enough for me. If I had been Judas or someone else in the crowd, I would have said, "This is the wrong Man to mess with. Did you see Him pick that man's ear up and slap it back on his head!"

But they took Jesus away to a mock trial, came to the decision to put Him to death, and handed Him over to Pilate. Peter failed when he cut off that servant's ear. But he fails again during this course of events and denies Jesus three times (Matt. 26:34, 35; Mark 14:30,72; Luke 22:34,61; John 13:38). It happened because Peter didn't pray.

Having a prayer life is the key to success with God. Every believer should learn how to pray scripturally and then do it. He shouldn't have to be forced to pray; praying is something he should do without coercion. If he really believes God hears and answers prayer, he will do it, and he will be faithful in prayer. God wants you to pray, not only to overcome temptation and the flesh, but to yield yourself to God so that He can bring you to new heights in your walk with Him.

In the next chapter, we will look in detail at what happens to Jesus in the final hours of His life on earth. We will see the heart of a Servant — the heart of the sinless Man who gave up His life for you and me.

Chapter 8
The Crucifixion of Jesus

In this chapter, we see the crucifixion of Jesus. We see the Son of God who came to this earth as a man to redeem mankind. In the ultimate example of servanthood, Jesus laid down His life for you and me. Let's read what happened.

> **MATTHEW 27:1-3**
> **1 When the morning was come, all the chief priests and elders of the people took counsel against Jesus to put him to death:**
> **2 And when they had bound him, they led him away, and delivered him to Pontius Pilate the governor.**
> **3 Then Judas, which had betrayed him, when he saw that he was condemned, repented himself. . . .**

After the fact, Judas understood that Satan had tricked him. After Satan used Judas for his purpose, he left, because the job was done. Then Judas came to his senses. He thought, *What have I done? I let Satan use me to condemn a just man.* Then Judas went out and killed himself (vv.4,5).

Satan will try to use you too. He will tell you that you can get more money if you do things a certain way. Then he will tell you that if it feels good, do it. And he will tell you to do it now because it will be more fun that way. He will tell you that it's okay to live with someone who isn't your husband or wife.

But, no, it's not all right; it's sin. If you fall for the devil's lies, failing to repent will be further opening yourself up to him. You might sit in church on Sunday, and you might even raise your hands, speak in tongues, and shout, "Hallelujah!" But you're not fooling God or the devil by your actions. They know what you're doing. Satan has his purpose for you, and it is to steal from you and to destroy your life. God has a purpose for you too. It's an eternal purpose with eternal blessing — on this earth and in Heaven. But you have to repent — turn from sin — and get right with Him to receive it.

Jesus Is Brought Before Pilate

Let's read what is happening to Jesus at this time.

MATTHEW 27:11-17
11 And Jesus stood before the governor: and the governor asked him, saying, Art thou the King of the Jews? And Jesus said unto him, Thou sayest.
12 And when he was accused of the chief priests and elders, he answered nothing.

13 Then said Pilate unto him, Hearest thou not how many things they witness against thee?

14 And he answered him to never a word; insomuch that the governor marvelled greatly.

15 Now at that feast the governor was wont to release unto the people a prisoner, whom they would.

16 And they had then a notable prisoner, called Barabbas.

17 Therefore when they were gathered together, Pilate said unto them, Whom will ye that I release unto you? Barabbas, or Jesus which is called Christ?

The crowd answered, "Barabbas!" when Pilate asked them which prisoner he should release. Remember, on the previous Sunday, this same crowd of people were throwing palm branches and their coats on the ground, shouting, "Hosanna to the Highest!" Just five days later, they're saying, "We don't want Him anymore. Turn Barabbas loose and crucify Jesus! That is how much we despise Him!"

There Are No Rewards For Being a Crowd-Pleaser

You can't live your life to please people. People are fickle; they will turn on you, sometimes before you can blink! If you are concerned with what your mama thinks, your daddy thinks, your sister thinks, your brother thinks, your friends think — if you want to be "cool" and "one of the crowd" in the eyes of society — at some point in time, you are going to be disappointed.

There is only One you can count on at all times, and it is God Almighty! He will be a friend when you are friendless. He will be a father when you are fatherless. He will be a mother when you are motherless. He will be your sister when you are sisterless. He will be your brother when you are brotherless. He will be your banker when your banker says, "No!" He will be your lawyer when you need one. He will be your friend in the courtroom who will witness for you. God is always on your side!

You'd better forget about trying to be cool. It would be better just to make Jesus the Lord of your life. Then obey God and do what He says for you to do. He is the only One you can count on over the long haul. He never changes.

In the end, you are going to stand before the One who hung on that tree — on the Cross of Calvary — for you. If you choose in life to go with the crowd, trying to be smooth, He is going to say to you, "So you wanted to be cool. You can't enter into eternal coolness."

The day is going to come when eternal life will be the coolest thing in town! And everybody is going to want to get in on it at that time. But only those who have heard the Lord's call, only those who have obeyed Him, will be able to get into the Kingdom. The Scripture says, "Wide is the road that leads to hell, and narrow is the gate that leads to life" (Matt. 7:13,14).

Make Your Choice Today!

Choose this day which way you will go! Are you going to choose Barabbas? Are you going to choose the world? Or are you going to take Jesus as King of kings and Lord of lords? Which way are you going to go?

Are you going to obey God or listen to everyone else's big mouth and their opinion? If I had listened to people's opinions, I would not be a pastor today, answering the call of God on my life. People told me that I was a fool to obey God. I decided to be a fool, and nobody is calling me a fool anymore! But if I had listened to man, the ministry I have today wouldn't exist. You can't afford to listen to flesh and blood. You'd better listen to the Holy One on the inside.

Pilate responded to the people's cries by saying, "I'm washing my hands of this Man. I find no fault in Him. I have nothing to do with this; send Him off " (Matt. 27:24).

The Soldiers Mock and Torture Jesus

Then the Roman soldiers took Jesus. The Bible says that they scourged Him (Matt. 27:26). While all of this was going on, Jesus never opened His mouth. He obeyed the will of the Father. He'd said earlier at the Mount of Olives, *"Thinkest thou that I cannot now pray to my Father, and he shall presently give me more than twelve legions of angels? But how then shall the scriptures be fulfilled, that thus it must be?"* (Matt. 26:53,54). But now He kept His mouth shut.

Those Roman soldiers then stripped off Jesus' garments so that He was naked. They began to mock Him. They put a purple robe on Him and took a crown of thorns and crushed it into His skull. Then the Bible says that they spit on His face. (*See* Matthew 27:27-31.)

Then the soldiers beat Him again and again and again. Isaiah chapter 52 says that His face and body were so beaten and bruised that He hardly resembled a human. In other words, what you had was a mob beating Jesus, and nobody helped pull them off of Him. They beat Him within an inch of His life.

In fact, the beating was so bad that He physically couldn't carry the Cross. He didn't have any strength left after receiving such brutal punishment. So they found a certain man and made him carry Jesus' Cross.

Let's read a description of this in the Book of Isaiah.

ISAIAH 53:3
3 He [Jesus] **is despised and rejected of men; a man of sorrows, and acquainted with grief: and we hid as it were our faces from him; he was despised, and we esteemed him not.**

The crowd was shouting, "Crucify Him! Do away with Him! Give us the murderer Barabbas!" These were the same people Jesus had healed and raised from the dead.

Isaiah 53:4 says, *"Surely he hath borne our griefs* [sicknesses, diseases, and pains], *and carried our sorrows: yet we did esteem him stricken, smitten of God, and afflicted."*

I'm telling you, as Jesus was being beaten, the crowd was yelling, "Put another lick on Him! Hit Him again!" I want you to see that it wasn't like what we see pictured in a Sunday school curriculum. Why did Jesus receive such a gruesome beating? *For you and for me*. He didn't deserve to be beaten. He had done nothing but bless and help people.

You and I were the ones who deserved the beating. But Jesus kept His mouth shut because He was thinking of you and me. During each blow, He was looking ahead and seeing us. We don't know how long this beating took place, but while it was happening, Jesus never said a word, because He was seeing you and me where we are today — and *every* person in the world who would accept His sacrifice and receive Him as Savior and Lord.

Isaiah 53:5 goes on to say, *"But he was wounded for OUR transgressions, he was bruised for OUR iniquities: the chastisement of OUR peace was upon him; and with his stripes WE are healed."*

The last thing the soldiers did before they put Jesus on the Cross was to whip Him. They made a whip like the ones used in slavery times in America, except this whip had rock, metal, and bone at the end of it. And every time the end of the lash hit Jesus' back, it ripped out a hunk of flesh.

The Bible says that with each stripe — with each chunk of flesh torn from Jesus' body — healing was being bought for flu, for cancer, for sickle-cell anemia, for AIDS, and for whatever could trouble you — for whatever could break your peace or destroy your life. First Peter 2:24 says, "By His stripes, you were healed."

Jesus' Love for You Motivated Him To Endure Suffering and Fulfill the Will of God

I want you to understand how much you are loved! Men have died for other men. Men have jumped on hand grenades and fallen on swords to save others in war. But never has there been a man who had never sinned, who had done only right, who loved people so much that He would premeditatedly take the punishment upon Himself that all of them deserved.

> **ISAIAH 53:6**
> 6 All we like sheep have gone astray; we have turned every one to his own way; and the Lord hath laid on him the iniquity of us all.

We all should have been crucified, and Jesus should have been the One doing the crucifying. But He reversed the table because He didn't want you to suffer a day! That is why we should not give in to sickness, disease, fear, lack, or anything else that is a result of sin. The price that was paid was so high.

Jesus' crucifixion was in the plan of God. It wasn't the Jews who killed Jesus. And it wasn't the Romans who did it. *God* had a plan to save you and me from the ravages of sin and the tyranny of Satan.

Remember we said in an earlier chapter that Jesus was God's seed in the earth. And we saw that, "*...Except a corn of wheat fall into the ground and die, it abideth alone: but if it die, it bringeth forth much fruit"* (John 12:24). God planted Jesus; the seed had to die on Good Friday.

Let's continue reading Matthew's account of Jesus' crucifixion.

> **MATTHEW 27:30-35,39,40**
> **30 And they spit upon him, and took the reed, and smote him on the head.**
> **31 And after that they had mocked him, they took the robe off from him, and put his own raiment on him, and led him away to crucify him.**
> **32 And as they came out, they found a man of Cyrene, Simon by name: him they compelled to bear his cross.**
> **33 And when they were come unto a place called Golgotha, that is to say, a place of a skull,**
> **34 They gave him vinegar to drink mingled with gall: and when he had tasted thereof, he would not drink.**
> **35 And they crucified him, and parted his garments, casting lots: that it might be fulfilled which was spoken by the prophet, They parted my**

garments among them, and upon my vesture did they cast lots. . . .

39 And they that passed by reviled him, wagging their heads,

40 And saying, Thou that destroyest the temple, and buildest it in three days, save thyself. If thou be the Son of God, come down from the cross.

In another Gospel account, it describes how they drove two-pound spikes through Jesus' hands and legs. They did this while He was on the ground; they drove those spikes through His body. Then they hung Him on the Cross.

Think about a hole in someone's hand so big that you could see light through it. That is what Jesus' hands looked like after His resurrection. Jesus said to Thomas when He appeared to him after the resurrection, "Reach here and put your fingers in the hole in My hand" (John 20:27).

After they nailed Jesus on the Cross, they lifted up the pole with His body on it and dropped the pole into the hole. When the pole hit the bottom of the hole, all of His joints were pulled out of place. It didn't break any of His bones, but the force of that jolt pulled them out of place.

Have you ever hit your funny bone? Do you remember what it feels like to hit your funny bone just once? The pain eventually subsides, but how do you think it feels to have every bone in your body dislocated? That is what happened to Jesus.

The Death of Jesus

The crucifixion of Jesus is not a pretty story. It is torture, pure and simple. Let's continue reading from Matthew's Gospel.

MATTHEW 27:35,36
35 And they crucified him, and parted his garments, casting lots: that it might be fulfilled which was spoken by the prophet, They parted my garments among them, and upon my vesture did they cast lots.
36 And sitting down they watched him there.

They all sat down! They were watching the show — Jesus' body bloodied from head to toe, dislocated and bruised. It's no wonder He didn't resemble a man. They set over His head the accusation Pilate had written: "...*THIS IS JESUS THE KING OF THE JEWS*" (Matt. 27:37). Then the chief priests, scribes, and elders walked by and said, "If He is the Son of God, let Him come on down off that Cross!" He is getting what He deserved. He said, 'I am the Son of God'" (Matt. 27:41-43). Even the thieves on both sides mocked Jesus (v. 44).

The whole world was against Jesus — the same world He came to save, heal, deliver, and bless! His disciples ran away and hid themselves. The only person who stayed around was His mother and a few women. John hugged Jesus' mother. And Jesus said to him, "This is your mother; take care of her" (John 19:25-27). Then John took her away from the hill.

Let's read about the final moments of Jesus' death.

> **MATTHEW 27:45,46**
> **45 Now from the sixth hour there was darkness over all the land unto the ninth hour.**
> **46 And about the ninth hour Jesus cried with a loud voice, saying, Eli, Eli, lama sabachthani? that is to say, My God, my God, why hast thou forsaken me?**

What happened at that moment in time from the sixth to the ninth hour? When Jesus was being beaten and bruised by those soldiers, He was bearing every sickness and disease. On the Cross, He was now being made sin for us. Suspended between Heaven and earth on that pole, Jesus bore the sin of mankind. Every filthy thing that could come to your mind was being pressed on Jesus — the depravity, the fear, the depression, and the shame of sin. And for the first time, He was separated from His Father. You see, God can't look at sin. For the first time, Jesus felt that separation.

Some of those who stood by filled a sponge with vinegar and put it on a reed to give Jesus a drink (Matt. 27:48). They said, "Let's see if the prophet Elijah comes to save Him" (v. 49). Then Jesus cried with a loud voice and gave up the ghost (v. 50).

Isaiah describes another facet of the final moments of Jesus just before and just after His crucifixion.

> **ISAIAH 53:7-9**
> **7 He was oppressed, and he was afflicted, yet he opened not his mouth: he is brought as a lamb to the slaughter, and as a sheep before her shearers is dumb, so he openeth not his mouth.**
> **8 He was taken from prison and from judgment: and who shall declare his generation? for he was cut off out of the land of the living: for the transgression of my people was he stricken.**
> **9 And he made his grave with the wicked, and with the rich in his death; because he had done no violence, neither was any deceit in his mouth.**

Notice verse 9. How did Jesus make His grave with the wicked? What does that mean? It doesn't mean that they took His body and put it in the hole with wicked people. It means something more than that. Psalm 9:17 says, *"The wicked shall be turned into hell, and all the nations that forget God."* Psalm

16:10 says, *"For thou wilt not leave my* [talking about Jesus] *soul in hell; neither wilt thou suffer thine Holy One to see corruption."* The Holy One who went to hell was Jesus! Jesus went to hell in our place!

The Scripture says, "He made His grave with the wicked" (Isa. 53:9). Unless somebody paid the price for us, hell is what you and I would receive. If Jesus hadn't gone to hell in our place — if He hadn't suffered the ravages of hell — the full penalty of our sin would not have been paid.

Jesus' grave was made with the wicked. Religion doesn't like this. They ask,"How can a holy God be taken into hell with the wicked?" *Because He was made to be sin!* Hell was the punishment for all who sinned. There isn't a person anywhere, except Jesus the Sinless One, who hasn't sinned. And by right and by the Law, everyone who's ever sinned was supposed to go to hell eternally. But Jesus was taken to hell itself to pay the price for us!

James 2:10 says, *"For whosoever shall keep the whole law, and yet offend in one point, he is guilty of all."* It wasn't enough that Jesus was beaten, that He bore our sicknesses and diseases, was crucified, and became sin on the Cross. He had to pay all the price! And part of the price was to enter hell on our behalf, in our stead. God's plan was that Jesus go to hell instead of us — so that we wouldn't have to!

Chapter 9
Hell Is a Real Place

Hell isn't a state of mind. It is a real place. There are people there right now — some of them you know. Don't join them! In the Bible, hell is described as a place of torment, where there is weeping, wailing, and gnashing of teeth (Matt. 8:12; 13:42,50; 22:13; 24:51; 25:30; Luke 13:28). We can read about hell as a place of torment in the account of the rich man and Lazarus.

LUKE 16:19-26
19 There was a certain rich man, which was clothed in purple and fine linen, and fared sumptuously every day:
20 And there was a certain beggar named Lazarus, which was laid at his gate, full of sores,
21 And desiring to be fed with the crumbs which fell from the rich man's table: moreover the dogs came and licked his sores.
22 And it came to pass, that the beggar died, and was carried by the angels into Abraham's bosom: the rich man also died, and was buried;
23 And in hell he lift up his eyes, BEING IN TORMENTS, and seeth Abraham afar off, and Lazarus in his bosom.
24 And he cried and said, Father Abraham, have mercy on me, and send Lazarus, that he may dip

> the tip of his finger in water, and cool my tongue;
> **FOR I AM TORMENTED IN THIS FLAME.**
> **25 But Abraham said, Son, remember that thou in
> thy lifetime receivedst thy good things, and
> likewise Lazarus evil things: but now he is
> comforted, and THOU ARE TORMENTED.**
> **26 And beside all this, between us and you there is
> a great gulf fixed: so that they which would pass
> from hence to you cannot; neither can they pass to
> us, that would come from thence.**

Lazarus, the poor beggar, was placed in Abraham's Bosom. Abraham's Bosom was where all the Old Testament saints went — Elijah, Elisha, Isaiah, Jeremiah, and all the rest of them. Before Jesus came to earth, people who believed God — who had faith in God — went to Abraham's Bosom.

You see, the Old Testament saints were not born again; their sins had not been washed away. Although they believed God, they couldn't go to Heaven. They were not new creations in Christ Jesus. But because they had faith in Christ, the coming Messiah, God placed them in what was called "Paradise" or "Abraham's Bosom" until the Holy One should come.

But this passage says that the wicked rich man went to hell. Psalm 9:17 says, *"THE WICKED SHALL BE TURNED INTO HELL, and all the nations that forget God."* There's no doubt about it.

The end result of the wicked is hell. Hell is not a vacation spot. It's a place of eternal damnation.

Friend, there is no such thing as purgatory. There isn't a place where the wicked can go for a certain number of years and then be released when they learn their lesson. No, hell is a place of eternity. If you go there, it's forever. You don't want to go there![1] But you don't have to. Jesus went in your stead. He paid the price so that you would never have to go to that awful place.

Let's continue reading the account of the rich man and Lazarus.

> **LUKE 16:23,24**
> **23 And in hell he** [the rich man] **lift up his eyes, being in TORMENTS, and seeth Abraham afar off, and Lazarus in his bosom.**
> **24 And he cried and said, Father Abraham, have mercy on me, and send Lazarus, that he may dip the tip of his finger in water, and cool my tongue; for I am tormented in this flame.**

Notice verse 23 says the word "torments" — plural. Hell is nothing but constant torments. It never stops, day in and day out. It's the most horrific place ever created. But it was not created for men; it was created as the end result of Satan and those of the heavenly host who followed Satan — the fallen angels. But if anyone wants to follow Satan, act like

Satan, live like Satan, and turn down God's salvation, then hell will be their final destination too.

Let's notice some other things about hell from this passage of Scripture in Luke 16. *First*, the rich man in hell recognized Lazarus who was in Abraham's Bosom. *So we know that there are memories in hell.* You will remember this very day if you go there. If you choose not to accept Jesus Christ as Savior, you will remember reading this book. You will remember my words and wished you had heeded them.

Second, this rich man had the same attitude he had on earth. He said, "Send that beggar to do something for me. Have him dip his finger in water and cool my tongue, because it's hot! I am tormented in this flame." Abraham's Bosom had to be close enough to where the rich man was in hell, because the rich man could see into Abraham's Bosom, and Lazarus in Abraham's Bosom could see into hell.

Third, not only did the rich man know who Lazarus was, he knew who Abraham was. And Abraham had been dead for one hundred years when this happened! *You see, in eternity everybody knows everybody.* The Bible says, "We will be known as we are known" (1 Cor. 13:12).

Let's read how Abraham responded to the rich man's request that Lazarus help him.

LUKE 16:26
26 ...between us and you there is a great gulf fixed: so that they which would pass from hence to you cannot; neither can they pass to us, that would come from thence.

The rich man responded, *"Then he said, I pray thee therefore, father, that thou wouldest send him to my father's house: For I have five brethren; that he may testify unto them, lest they also come into this place of torment"* (vv. 27,28).

Abraham answered, "They have the Law. They have Moses and the prophets. Let them hear and heed them" (v. 29).

The rich man thought that if someone was raised from the dead and went to tell his brothers to repent, they would surely believe then (v. 30). But Abraham said, *"...If they hear not Moses and the prophets, neither will they be persuaded, though one rose from the dead"* (v. 31).

So you see, hell is a place where people go. Jesus had to go there in order for us to be redeemed and have our sins washed away. He had to suffer in the flames. He had to suffer the indignity that Satan and his cohorts heaped on Him while He was there.

For three days, Jesus suffered untold agony for us! (But I want you to know, there is good news at the end.)

When Jesus went to hell, I believe there was both glee and Pandemonium. All those demons were down there partying! No doubt, they said, "We have the Holy One! He is defeated! It took us three years, but now, man on earth is our slave forever."

Jesus' Death Was Not the End!

Moses and the Old Testament saints were there in hell (a part of hell called Abraham's Bosom) watching Jesus being tortured in the flames by Satan and his cohorts. But Satan and those demons didn't know what was going on. They didn't realize that the worst thing that could happen to them was for the Son of God to be there in that place. But they would see that Jesus would defeat death, hell, and the grave and pay the complete price for you and me.

The beatings didn't kill Jesus. The soldiers didn't kill Him. The sickness and disease didn't kill Him. Jesus said in John 10:17, *"Therefore doth my Father love me, because I LAY DOWN MY LIFE, that I might take it again."*

Most people stop at Jesus' crying with a loud voice and giving up the ghost (Matt. 27:50). But there's more. Certainly, we can refer the Cross as the end of Jesus' physical ministry on earth. But if everything stopped at the Cross, we would be in trouble.

The Cross was only the beginning. It wasn't the place of victory per se, but without the Cross, there would be no victory. *Victory for us came by way of the Cross.* People wear cross symbols as jewelry, and that's all right because of the victory that ensued after Jesus' crucifixion. But there is another symbol we should commemorate as well — the empty tomb!

[1] For further study along this line, *see* Bishop Butler's book *Hell: You Don't Want To Go There.*

Chapter 10
Resurrection Sunday!

In this chapter, we will look at the victory Jesus obtained for us through His death, burial, and resurrection. Jesus suffered on the Cross and died. But, praise God, it didn't end there. The Cross appeared to be a place of defeat, but in dying on the Cross, Jesus was fulfilling God's plan to redeem mankind — to save us from death, hell, and the grave. Let's read what remarkable things happened after Jesus' death.

MATTHEW 27:50-54

50 Jesus, when he had cried again with a loud voice, yielded up the ghost.

51 And, behold, the veil of the temple was rent in twain from the top to the bottom; and the earth did quake, and the rocks rent;

52 And the graves were opened; and many bodies of the saints which slept arose,

53 And came out of the graves after his resurrection, and went into the holy city, and appeared unto many.

54 Now when the centurion, and they that were with him, watching Jesus, saw the earthquake, and those things that were done, they feared greatly, saying, Truly this was the Son of God.

After he saw the earthquake, the veil of the temple being torn from top to bottom, and dead people getting up out of their graves, the centurion and his soldiers said, "Truly, this was the Son of God!"

I think I might have said that too! I mean, can you imagine hearing about all the things Jesus had done and then, all of a sudden, seeing your Uncle Joe, who's been dead and buried for twenty years, walking toward you? That would make you say, "Truly this was the Son of God!"

Jesus Reconciled Us to the Father

In the last chapter, we learned that Jesus paid the whole price for us — He was crucified; He died and was buried; He went to hell and defeated Satan, taking from him the keys of death and hell (Rev. 1:18); and He rose from the dead! In Jesus' death, burial, and resurrection, God consummated His great plan of redemption to restore mankind to Himself — to restore to him his lost place of relationship and fellowship with the Father.

Let's read more about this blessed reconciliation.

2 CORINTHIANS 5:17-21
17 Therefore if any man be in Christ, he is a new creature: old things are passed away; behold, all things are become new.
18 And all things are of God, who hath reconciled us to himself by Jesus Christ, and hath given to us the ministry of reconciliation;
19 To wit, that God was in Christ, reconciling the world unto himself, not imputing their trespasses unto them; and hath committed unto us the word of reconciliation.
20 Now then we are ambassadors for Christ, as though God did beseech you by us: we pray you in Christ's stead, be ye reconciled to God.
21 For he hath made him to be sin for us, who knew no sin; THAT WE MIGHT BE MADE THE RIGHTEOUSNESS OF GOD IN HIM.

Jesus became sin for us! Why did He do it? So that we might be made the very righteousness of God!

Hebrews 9:22 says, *"And almost all things are by the law purged with blood; and without shedding of blood is no remission."* Everything has to be cleansed in blood. The only way you and I could be delivered was for Someone with untainted blood die in our place — Someone who would qualify to be the substitutionary sacrifice for you and me.

You see, every person born after Adam was born with the nature of sin. When Adam and Eve sinned, they died spiritually at that moment. We know that

Adam lived 930 years after that, but he died spiritually the moment he sinned. Spiritual death is the parent of physical death.

When God told Adam and Eve that if they ate of a certain tree, they would surely die, God was referring to spiritual death. Spiritual death is receiving Satan's nature and being separated from God. And that is exactly what happened when they ate from that tree. When Adam and Eve sinned, they received the nature of Satan. Their blood became tainted.

So every person born after Adam and Eve was born with the nature of sin in their bloodstream. Man is the carrier. You can't be born without a daddy, and your daddy has the nature of sin in his blood.

When Adam sinned and sin was introduced to the human race, Satan thought he had everybody; he thought he had the planet locked up. But God had a better idea. He had a plan. The Holy Spirit would overshadow the virgin Mary, and that holy thing that would be born unto her would be born without sin (Luke 1:35). Jesus' blood was pure. And because His blood was pure, His blood was what was required to wash away our sins.

As I said before, there have been men who have shed their blood for other men. There have been men who died in battle for others. They may have saved the physical bodies of others for a time, but these men could do nothing for the eternal state of man.

But the blood of Jesus was *clean blood*! Therefore, that blood could be used to wipe away our real problem — the problem of spiritual death. Spiritual death in its final form is eternal death in hell forever!

So without the shedding of blood, there is no way to wipe away sin. That is why Jesus had to hang on that Cross and shed His blood. That is why they beat Him until blood came out of every part of Him. There was blood on the pole and on the dirt; there was blood everywhere. And when God saw the blood, He smiled. Everyone else was horrified at the sight of the blood, but when God saw it, He was glad, because that blood was what was required to save you and me.

Jesus Suffered Separation From God

Isaiah 53:6 says, *"All we like sheep have gone astray; we have turned every one to his own way; and the Lord hath laid on him the iniquity of us all."* The word "iniquity" means *lawlessness, unrighteousness*, and *wickedness*. Remember when

Jesus was on that Cross and screamed, "My God, why have You forsaken Me?" At that very moment, God laid on Jesus every sin you and I ever committed — every thought and action of every sin that would ever be committed — and separated Himself from the Son.

As I said, God can't look at sin. So the Father turned His back on the Son and for the first time in Jesus' existence, He was separated from God. He felt the separation between Him and God. Why would God do that to His only Son, and why would Jesus allow that to happen? *For you and me!* God laid on Jesus the sin of us all.

Jesus Kicked Satan's Behind!

Jesus was crucified on Good Friday. As I said, His crucifixion looked like a defeat, but it meant eternal victory for you and me. I tell you, Good Friday should make you more committed. People "turn over new leafs," make resolutions, and try to start life afresh and anew at the start of a new year. But Good Friday should really make you want to turn over a new leaf! When you realize what Jesus went through, you won't be saying, "Lord, You wait till I'm ready to serve You; I'm not ready for You yet," you'll be saying, "Lord, here I am. Thank You for saving me. I owe you my life." You won't have the attitude, *I'm going to do what I want to do, and when I'm done, I'll think about serving the Lord. Or maybe I'll wait till I'm on my deathbed to ask to get into His Kingdom.* You will know that *God* isn't indebted to *you*; *you* are indebted to *Him*.

We know Jesus was resurrected on the third day. Let's read what really happened on that glorious Sunday morning.

HEBREWS 1:1,2,6-9
1 God, who at sundry times and in divers manners spake in time past unto the fathers by the prophets,
2 Hath in these last days spoken unto us by his Son, whom he hath appointed heir of all things, by whom also he made the worlds. . . .
6 And again, when he bringeth in the firstbegotten into the world, he saith, And let all the angels of God worship him.
7 And of the angels he saith, Who maketh his angels spirits, and his ministers a flame of fire.
8 But unto the Son he saith, Thy throne, O God, is for ever and ever: a sceptre of righteousness is the sceptre of thy kingdom.
9 Thou hast loved righteousness, and hated iniquity; therefore God, even thy God, hath anointed thee with the oil of gladness above thy fellows.

This passage of Scripture is talking about Sunday morning. Jesus was there in the very pit of hell for you and me. But in the high court of Heaven, God the Father began to speak, "Thy throne, O God…" Elsewhere in the Scripture, it says that it rumbled in there. It was like an earthquake in hell.

Satan and his cohorts were partying in hell, thinking they had Jesus. Satan was laughing as he watched Jesus suffer. But then they heard that thunderous burst that shook the walls of hell. They heard, "Thy throne, O God, is forever. A scepter of righteousness is the scepter of Thy Kingdom." Everything stopped cold in hell. The party stopped. The music stopped. Everything stopped. And Satan said, "Oh, no! I've heard that Voice before. That is the Voice that kicked me out of Heaven."

Satan heard God say, *"Thou hast loved righteousness, and hated iniquity; therefore God, even they God, hath ANOINTED THEE with the oil of gladness above thy fellows"* (Heb. 1:9). And when the Father said, "anointed thee," the Holy Ghost said, "That is My cue." And the Holy Ghost energized Jesus, and Jesus began to make a wreck out of Satan!

Colossians 2:15 says, *"And having spoiled principalities and powers, he* [Jesus] *made a shew of them openly, triumphing over them in it."* The word "spoiled" is blind to us today. We would say, "Having kicked their behind, Jesus spoiled principalities and powers!" We could say that Jesus kicked Satan's behind!

There in hell began the greatest victory ever in the history of the planet. There in hell was the biggest fight anyone has ever seen. All the demons tried to take Jesus. But Jesus prevailed because He was anointed with the oil of gladness — the Holy Ghost! He slammed principalities against the wall. He slammed powers against the wall. He walked up to Satan and slammed him on the ground. He took the keys of death, hell, and the grave from him and said, "All power is given unto Me in Heaven and earth" (Matt. 28:18).

The greatest beating that ever was took place there. I wish I could have been there to see it! But I want you to know that those in Abraham's Bosom did see it! Moses saw it. Abraham saw it. David saw it. And they began to praise God when they saw Jesus the Victor conquer Satan.

Once Jesus paid the price, the high court of Heaven said, "That is enough!" Jesus won in hell, but that was not the end. Jesus took the keys of death, hell, and the grave and went right back up to the surface. He went back to earth to pick up His body.

Jesus Returned to Earth After His Resurrection

Remember you are a spirit being, not a body. You are a spirit; you have a soul; and you live in a body (1 Thess. 5:23). You are a spirit being that possesses a soul while living in a physical body. Jesus was no different. The real Jesus was in the pit of hell while His body was in the tomb.

Jesus conquered Satan in the pit of hell. Then He preached the Gospel to those spirits in Abraham's Bosom. He emptied Abraham's Bosom (Eph. 4:8) and went back up to the surface.

Let's read what happened when Jesus returned to earth.

> **JOHN 20:11-17**
> 11 But Mary stood without at the sepulchre weeping: and as she wept, she stooped down, and looked into the sepulchre,
> 12 And seeth two angels in white sitting, the one at the head, and the other at the feet, where the body of Jesus had lain.
> 13 And they say unto her, Woman, why weepest thou? She saith unto them, Because they have taken away my Lord, and I know not where they have laid him.
> 14 And when she had thus said, she turned herself back, and saw Jesus standing, and knew not that it was Jesus.

15 Jesus saith unto her, Woman, why weepest thou? whom seekest thou? She, supposing him to be the gardener, saith unto him, Sir, if thou have borne him hence, tell me where thou hast laid him, and I will take him away.

16 Jesus saith unto her, Mary. She turned herself, and saith unto him, Rabboni; which is to say, Master.

17 Jesus saith unto her, Touch me not; for I am not yet ascended to my Father: but go to my brethren, and say unto them, I ascend unto my Father, and your Father; and to my God, and your God.

In other words, Jesus said, "Don't touch Me yet, Mary." She saw Him standing in that tomb, alive, and He didn't want her to touch Him yet. He was just stopping by to pick up His body! He had not yet ascended to the Father to fulfill His priestly duties. (He would let Mary and the disciples touch Him later. I'll talk more about that in the next chapter.)

Then Jesus went to Thomas and the other disciples. They were worried; they thought they would be killed next. Jesus walked into the room and said, "Thomas, reach with your finger and put it in the holes of My hands. Take your hand and put it in the hole in My side. Be not faithless; only believe" (John 20:27). You see, Thomas had heard that Jesus had risen from the dead, but he didn't believe it.

Then Thomas said to Jesus, "My Lord and my God" (John 20:28).

Jesus said, ". . . *Thomas, because thou hast seen me, thou hast believed: blessed are they that have not seen, and yet have believed*" (John 20:29).

I haven't seen the Lord with my physical eyes, but I have seen Him with my spiritual eyes. I believe He is the risen Savior, Redeemer, and Lord. I believe and I am blessed. He said that I'm blessed, and I will take that! I accept it. What about you?

Chapter 11
The Finished Work Of Jesus Christ

Jesus is seated at the right hand of the Father today. He died for us, went to hell for us, defeated Satan for us, and now wants us to enforce what He has already accomplished. Let's look at what Jesus has done for us — what we have now as a result of His shed blood.

Jesus Our High Priest

Jesus wouldn't let the disciples touch Him after He had risen from the dead. He hadn't fulfilled His priestly duty yet. He hadn't gone into the Holy of Holies — into the Presence of God — and offered His blood on the Mercy Seat.

Let's read about Jesus as our High Priest in Hebrews chapter 9.

HEBREWS 9:12
12 Neither by the blood of goats and calves, but by his own blood he entered in once into the holy place, having obtained eternal redemption for us.

Every year the Old Testament high priest went into the temple of God where God resided. The priest took the blood of the sacrificed bulls and goats, sprinkled that blood on the mercy seat, and then counted that blood as sufficient to cover the sins of the people. Every year, he had to come back and do it again.

If the high priest walked into the Holy of Holies and wasn't purified himself — if he had sin in his life — he died right there. The high priest's robe had bells sewn at the bottom, and he had a rope tied around his ankles. As long as the people heard him clanging around in there, they knew he must be clean. But if they heard something hit the floor, then they pulled on the rope which was tied to his ankles to bring his body out. Nobody could go in there or they would die too. That is why Jesus wouldn't let Mary touch Him. He couldn't touch anything unclean, and Mary was still unclean.

According to Hebrews 9:12, Jesus went into the Holy of Holies once. You see, the blood of bulls and goats couldn't do the job. That blood was only a temporary solution; it only *covered* sins. But the blood of Jesus *removes* sin.

Let me give you an illustration along this line. Think about a time when you told your child to make up his bed. He might have had toys, crumbs, and all kinds of things under the covers. But he sort of straightens it up and covers up all that stuff and says, "Mama, I cleaned the bed." And you come in there and see all those lumps through the covers. He just *covered* the mess.

That is all the blood of bulls and goats did. It just covered the mess man was in. But Jesus' blood didn't cover sin; His blood *eradicated* sin! Jesus' blood obliterated sin! Jesus' blood washed away all sin so that there was not one speck left. And His blood was so powerful that it only had to be done one time.

So Jesus went into the Holy Place to offer His blood on the mercy seat. Now God the Father could have done one of two things: He could have accepted the blood Jesus shed in our stead, or He could have rejected it. Jesus put His blood on the mercy seat, bowed down before the Father, and the Father accepted the blood of Jesus in our place. Thank God that He accepted the blood, because if He hadn't, all of us would be doomed for hell!

Jesus' Blood Not Only Cleansed Us, It Gave Us Spiritual Authority

The price has been paid. Our sins have been washed away. Just having our sin washed away would have been enough! Freedom from hell would have been enough! To be able to live forever, eternally with God, would have been enough! But God did something else for us. Why would He do anything else for us? We didn't deserve anything. But God said, "No, I want to do more than just save them from hell."

Let's read what God did for us.

> **HEBREWS 10:12,13**
> **12 But this man** [Jesus], **after he had offered one sacrifice for sins for ever, sat down on the right hand of God;**
> **13 From henceforth expecting till his enemies be made his footstool.**

The Father received the blood of Jesus. Jesus is now sitting down next to the Father. Verse 13 says Jesus is expecting His enemies to be totally annihilated. Well, if He just sat down, then who is going to do all that? Who is going to continue to keep the devil underfoot? We are!

God had such confidence in us, the Body of Christ, that Jesus sat down and said, "They are going to make the devil my footrest! They are going to slam him so bad! And I'm just going to rest." Jesus did the real work in His death, burial, and resurrection. And He only had to do it one time. He defeated Satan, and we are to continually enforce that defeat.

How God Sees You

How God sees you is different from how you see yourself. Hebrews 10:14 says, *"For by one offering HE HATH PERFECTED for ever them that are sanctified."* God sees you as perfect! When you receive Jesus — when you make Him Lord of your life — God sees you as perfect! He doesn't see you like you see yourself, with your blemishes, mistakes, and problems! When God looks at you through the Blood, He sees you as being perfect from head to toe. No more blemishes; no more mess-ups! He sees you as being perfected forever!

That is the only way you could get into Heaven — to be perfect, sinless. There isn't anything in Heaven that God doesn't think is perfect. In the eyes of God, the blood of Jesus was so powerful, so forceful and dominating, that all who receive Jesus have been made perfect. They've been made perfect through the Blood!

Someone said, "But I don't deserve that." That's right, you *don't* deserve that. But God did it, anyway. God said, "I count them as being perfect." And when He talks about you, He talks about you as if you were perfect.

I didn't say you were perfect; *God* says you're perfect! Romans 4:17 says that God, *"...calleth those things which be not as though they were."* Hebrews 10:19 says, *"Having therefore, brethren, BOLDNESS to enter into the holiest by the blood of Jesus."* In other words, since God calls you perfect, you can boldly go to the throne anytime you want to. You don't need a priest or somebody else to get to God for you. No! Perfection can walk up to perfection and say, "Father, in the Name of Jesus…" And God will say, "Yes, My son." That Blood is so powerful that God sees you as perfect!

Second Corinthians 5:21 says, *"For he hath made him to be sin for us, who knew no sin; that we might be made the righteousness of God in him."* God has made us righteous in His eyes. There was no way we could be righteous except by the Blood. Through the Blood, we have been declared righteous, holy, sanctified, and *perfect*!

Sometimes when we mess up, we say, "God, look at me!"

And the Lord says, "I'm not looking at you; I'm looking at the Blood that's washed you."

We say, "But God, I messed up in the past."

He says, "Yes, but did you confess it?"

And if we did, God says, "Then you are perfect!"

Whether we feel perfect or not, God said it is so! He didn't say anything about His making us to *feel* perfect. He just said, "You're perfect," and that's that. Just as He said, "Light, be," and light was (Gen. 1:3), we have been made perfect, because God said, "You're perfect." We are perfect through the blood of Jesus.

Jesus Left Us an Inheritance

Naturally speaking, parents make a will as a vehicle to provide their children — their heirs — with an inheritance. I have heirs — a son and two daughters. And I have a will. That will expressly declares my children as my heirs and as beneficiaries of my assets, my possessions.

The New Testament is the last will and testament of the Lord Jesus Christ. Jesus wrote a will. And in that will — in the New Testament — is everything that belongs to Jesus. The Bible says that we are joint-heirs with Jesus Christ. Romans 8:16 and 17 says, *"The Spirit itself* [or Himself] *beareth witness with our spirit, that we are the children of God: AND IF CHILDREN, THEN HEIRS; heirs of God, and joint-heirs with Christ...."*

What does that passage mean? It means that everything Jesus gets, we get! Now if we get everything Jesus gets, we'd better find out what

Jesus gets. Let's study our inheritance — what belongs to us.

> **PHILIPPIANS 2:5-11**
> **5 Let this mind be in you, which was also in Christ Jesus:**
> **6 Who, being in the form of God, thought it not robbery to be equal with God:**
> **7 But made himself of no reputation, and took upon him the form of a servant, and was made in the likeness of men:**
> **8 And being found in fashion as a man, he humbled himself, and became obedient unto death, even the death of the cross.**
> **9 Wherefore GOD ALSO HATH HIGHLY EXALTED HIM, AND GIVEN HIM A NAME WHICH IS ABOVE EVERY NAME:**
> **10 That AT THE NAME OF JESUS EVERY KNEE SHOULD BOW, of things in heaven, and things in earth, and things under the earth;**
> **11 And that every tongue should confess that Jesus Christ is Lord, to the glory of God the Father.**

All three worlds — Heaven, earth, and hell — bow their knee to Jesus! Everything in the earth has a name. Sickness has a name. Poverty has a name. Fear has a name. Depression has a name. Every name and every knee must bow to the Name of Jesus. And not only does every name bow to Jesus, but it must also bow to any believer who speaks Jesus' Name in faith.

Poverty has to bow to you. Sickness has to bow to you. Depression has to bow to you. They all have to bow down to you! They all have to get on their knee. God gave that position of authority to you. You have been highly exalted. You're not just an old sinner saved by grace; you aren't just trying to get by somehow in these last days. No, you have been highly exalted. You have been perfected. When you speak, things happen!

Let's read a passage of Scripture in Isaiah that we already read in an earlier chapter.

ISAIAH 53:7-10

7 He [Jesus] was oppressed, and he was afflicted, yet he opened not his mouth: he is brought as a lamb to the slaughter, and as a sheep before her shearers is dumb, so he openeth not his mouth.

8 He was taken from prison and from judgment: and who shall declare his generation? for he was cut off out of the land of the living: for the transgression of my people was he stricken.

9 And he made his grave with the wicked, and with the rich in his death; because he had done no violence, neither was any deceit in his mouth.

10 Yet it pleased the Lord to bruise him; he hath put him to grief: when thou shalt make his soul an offering for sin, he shall see his seed, he shall prolong his days, and the pleasure of the Lord shall prosper in his hand.

God does everything through one method: seedtime and harvest. The only way to receive anything in the Kingdom of God is to plant. God did it first; He planted Jesus. He made Jesus an offering for sin. Read verse 10 again: "...*it PLEASED the Lord to bruise him; HE HATH PUT HIM TO GRIEF: when thou shalt make his soul an offering for sin, he shall see his seed, he shall prolong his days, and the pleasure of the Lord shall prosper in his hand.*"

When Jesus was hanging on that Cross screaming, "My God, My God, why have You forsaken Me," it didn't horrify the Father; it gratified Him. When Jesus was suffering in hell, it didn't horrify the Father; it gratified Him. Why? He was satisfied because the Son was being obedient. He was satisfied because He was looking at you and me. He was seeing that His seed — Jesus — was being planted and put in position to reap all of us into the Kingdom, causing us to become sons of God, just like Jesus.

Let's continue reading in Isaiah about God's Seed, Jesus.

ISAIAH 53:11,12
11 He shall see of the travail of his soul, and shall be satisfied: by his knowledge shall my righteous

servant justify many; for he shall bear their iniquities.

12 Therefore WILL I DIVIDE HIM A PORTION WITH THE GREAT, and HE SHALL DIVIDE THE SPOIL WITH THE STRONG. . . .

First, who are "the great" being referred to in verse 12? *You* are the great! Not only does God call you perfect, God calls you "the great"! *Then* God calls you "the strong"!

God also says that you get to have a portion of the spoil. Remember, everything that Jesus gets, you get! The whole earth belongs to Jesus. Jesus inherited what He received. Then God said Jesus was going to divide it! Everything that belongs to Jesus must be divided with you — you *perfect* one, you *great* one, you *strong* one!

Someone said, "But I don't *look* like the great."

Yes, but God says you are!

"Well, I'm a ninety-eight-pound weakling. I can't be the strong."

But God says you are! God is stronger than your weight. You are "the strong" in Jesus. Never again say, "I don't know what I'm going to do. I don't know how I'm going to make it." God made you the great. He made you the strong. He made you perfect before Him, and Satan knows it. The problem is, *we* don't know it. We're still thinking we're "dirty old sinners." But we aren't sinners! We've received an inheritance. We're perfect in Jesus' strength! We're rulers, conquerors, and overcomers! God has made us such.

We Are To Rule and Reign as Kings

Revelation 1:5 says, *"And from Jesus Christ, who is the faithful witness, and the first begotten of the dead...."* You see, Jesus used to be the only begotten Son of God (John 3:16). But He isn't the only begotten Son anymore. The word "begotten" means *born.* If there is a *first* begotten, there is a *second* begotten and a *third* begotten and so on. I don't know what number I am, but I'm one of those begotten!

If you are born again, then whatever Jesus gets, you get! He is the heir, and you are an heir. He is the Son, and you are a son. He is the perfect, and you are the perfect. He is the great, and you are the great. He is the strong, and you are the strong. You are all these things in Him — all because God accepted and received His blood.

Now let's look at another part of Revelation 1:5: *"And from Jesus Christ, who is the faithful witness, and the first begotten of the dead, AND THE*

PRINCE OF THE KINGS OF THE EARTH...."
First, notice the phrase, "...of the earth...." Jesus is
the Prince of the kings of the earth, not of Heaven.
Then notice it says "kings" — plural. There is not
just one king or two kings on the earth; there are
many kings! One "characteristic" of kingship is that
a king rules. He speaks, and what he says comes to
pass. Well, you are born of God, and God made you
a king!

Anybody who thinks God wants you — His
perfected, great, strong, joint-heir with Jesus Christ —
sick, broke, poor, and down is confused. God doesn't
want you sick, poor, and down-and-out. If He did,
why in the world did He make you perfect? Why did
He make you strong? Why did He make you great?
Why did He make you a king of the earth?

Since you are a king of the earth, it's about time
you started acting like a king. The Lord is on your
side. The enemy may come in like a flood, but the
Spirit of the Lord will bring a standard against him
(Isa. 59:19). Kings are not subjects. Kings *have*
subjects. And our subjects are the principalities and
powers in the sense that when you sit down on your
throne to reign, they can't do one thing but bow!

Sickness, poverty, and depression all have to
bow in front of Jesus and in front of you. It's about
time you started talking to your "subjects" because

of what Jesus did on Resurrection Day — when He shed His blood, rose from the grave, and defeated principalities and powers. God made you a king; it's time you stand up and take your plaee!

We Are Kings *and* Priests

Let's finish reading the passage of Scripture in Revelation.

> **REVELATION 1:5-7**
> **5 ... Unto him that loved us, and washed us from our sins in his own blood,**
> **6 And hath MADE US KINGS AND PRIESTS UNTO GOD and his Father; to him be glory and dominion for ever and ever. Amen.**
> **7 Behold, he cometh with clouds; and every eye shall see him, and they also which pierced him: and all kindreds of the earth shall wail because of him. Even so. Amen.**

Not only are you a king, but you are also a high priest. This verse is not just for the pastors, evangelists, prophets, apostles, and teachers. No, everyone who is born again is a priest unto God. Priests can walk into the Holy of Holies; they can go before God. Priests have fellowship with God. An Old Testament priest couldn't go before God until he was holy, without one shred of sin. Well, God has made you a priest! He has made you holy!

Someone said, "Preacher, you're going too far calling us holy. How dare you call us holy! The Bible says that our righteousness is as filthy rags [Isa. 64:6]."

Yes, the Bible says that. But none of what I'm teaching is about "us" and "ours" — it's about "Him" and "His"! When you receive Jesus Christ as your Lord and Savior, you take part in *His* righteousness, *His* Name, and *His* reward. It all comes to you because you become a son. To think anything less and to settle for anything less is to do a disservice to the blood of Jesus. It's time you get your chin off the ground, so to speak, and stop feeling sorry for yourself — sad, mad, and bad! Remember what Jesus has done for you. You are made a king and a priest, and the Lord is on your side!

Look at the phrase, *"And HATH made us kings and priests unto God..."* in verse 6. Before you were born, God set aside for you what you needed in order to be a priest in this earth — to be able to handle the holy things of God. What did He have prepared for you? The Name of Jesus, the Word of God, the blood of Jesus, faith, righteousness, peace, and joy. Then God did it — He made you a priest!

Our Priesthood Was Bestowed

What did we do to be honored by God with all of this? *Nothing!* That is why they call this message the Gospel. The word "Gospel" means *Good News.* The story of the Bible isn't about God being mad at you, beating you up, or God being some Judge who wants to smash you! No! A thousand times, no! The story of the Gospel is that God took nobodies like me and you who were on their way to hell and said, "I'm going to fix them up. I'm going to hook them up with Me."

God said to us, "First, I'm going to clean you up. I have to pour the Blood over you to wash off your filth and sin. Then I'm going to make you My son. All that I have — the whole universe — belongs to Me. The cattle on a thousand hills belong to Me [Ps. 50:10]. And since all of this belongs to Me, and you are My son, it belongs to you. I'm going to put you on the earth. I'm going to make you 'god' on the earth.

"In fact, I will give you such power that when you decree something according to what is written in My Word, it will be so. And although there are spiritual enemies walking around there, unless you let them, they can't hurt you! This is what I say about you, and what I speak always comes to pass. You are perfected! You are sanctified! You are great!

You are strong! You are a priest, a king, and a son. Now go to it! I'm sitting down. You take care of business!"

When we stand up for what belongs to us in Christ Jesus and refuse to quit, all hell trembles. This is what God intended for His body of believers on earth — that we would rule and reign on earth as kings because of what Jesus accomplished for us.

When I personally think about what the Lord has done for me — about His great plan of redemption and Jesus' consummation of that plan in His death, burial, and resurrection — my hands have to go up in praise, and I have to say, "Thank You!" I have to bow down on my knee and say, "Thank You for all You've done for me. Thank You for setting me free, for making a way for me. You have given me so much. I can't walk in this earth defeated. I can never give up. I can never put You down by giving in to defeat, by calling myself names, or by calling my brothers and sisters names."

There's only one word to describe what the Lord has given you: *victory*! When you speak, devils tremble, and the earth shakes. Jesus is your Lord, Savior, Master, Healer, Provider. Let the Word of God become more to you than words on paper. When God says you're great, you are! When He says you're strong, you are! So when the devil tells you, "You can't win," you tell him, "I've *already* won!"

What Jesus did has been done. It's not what's going to happen in the future; it's what God has already done for us in Christ.

Jesus Did the Work, But the Responsibility Is Ours

What are we going to do with Jesus' last week? We saw the final moments of His life unfold, as He shared important truths from the heart of God — truths that He wanted to be sure people remembered after He left. Then we saw Jesus, the Word made flesh, become the final Sacrifice for mankind, redeeming us from the clutches of sin, sickness, death, hell, and the grave.

Jesus' last week was a momentous one, and that's an understatement! Because He submitted to the will of God and obeyed Him to the letter — even up to the moment of His death when He laid down His life for us — we have everlasting life and everything that life entails today.

Other Titles By Keith A. Butler Sr. And Word of Faith Publishing

Bishop Keith A. Butler

A Seed Will Meet Any Need	BK003
Hell: You Don't Want To Go There	BK005
Making Room for Yourself	BK007
Angels — God's Servants for You	BK010
Success Strategies From Heaven	BK001 (Harrison House, Inc.)
What On Earth Are We Here For?	BK002 (Harrison House, Inc.)

Min. Deborah L. Butler

Establishing Godly Relationships Through Marriage and Family	BK012

Rev. Keith A. Butler II

God's Plan for the Single Saint	BK006

▶ The Internet. It has the potential to communicate information and connect people in powerful ways.

Now it is bringing together Kenneth Hagin, Kenneth Copeland, Keith Butler, Jesse Duplantis, Creflo Dollar, Jerry Savelle, Mac Hammond, and many more for something historic... something with exciting possibilities for you, your family, and the world.

THE TIME HAS COME

"Now you can join the online revolution, build your faith, protect your family and be a part of taking the Gospel to the world."

CFAITH.com
▶ YOUR INTERCONNECTED FAITH FAMILY

These well-respected ministries, along with many others, are uniting to connect the global faith family and reach out to others with the life-changing message of faith through the power of the Internet. They are coming together to launch **CFAITH.com**.